Thinking Allowed

Eurisko

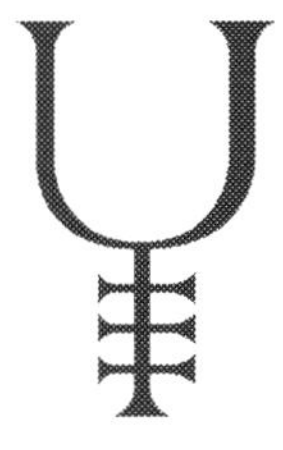

What you weren't taught at university: (Almost) everything you need to know about building a better optical business.

JULIAN WILES

authorHOUSE®

AuthorHouse™ UK
1663 Liberty Drive
Bloomington, IN 47403 USA
www.authorhouse.co.uk
Phone: 0800.197.4150

© 2016 Julian Wiles. All rights reserved.

No part of this book may be reproduced, stored in a retrieval system, or transmitted by any means without the written permission of the author.

Published by AuthorHouse 08/01/2016

ISBN: 978-1-5246-3310-3 (sc)
ISBN: 978-1-5246-3308-0 (hc)
ISBN: 978-1-5246-3309-7 (e)

Print information available on the last page.

Any people depicted in stock imagery provided by Thinkstock are models, and such images are being used for illustrative purposes only.
Certain stock imagery © Thinkstock.

This book is printed on acid-free paper.

Because of the dynamic nature of the Internet, any web addresses or links contained in this book may have changed since publication and may no longer be valid. The views expressed in this work are solely those of the author and do not necessarily reflect the views of the publisher, and the publisher hereby disclaims any responsibility for them.

CONTENTS

HELLO

Before *Thinking Allowed*, there has never been a book written for precisely where you are today – and that is why you are invited to read it. This is the book you should read before spending a single penny on your next step to building a better optical business.

Within, you'll find some of the secrets they didn't teach you at university – secrets you need to know if you want to build a better optical business faster. It might save you money and get you to where you want to be quicker than you thought possible. *Thinking Allowed* will make sure that you start from the place that is relevant to you. The most important thing is implementing your ideas, and this is the difference you need to succeed in a competitive world.

You'll learn how to generate new, profitable, and sustainable revenue streams today, tomorrow, and in the future. You'll be able to create a blueprint that will future-proof your business and help you maximise your professional and clinical skills. This new plan will allow you to make everything you can out of everything you've got. There is no secret formula expressed in large letters and small numbers and graceful parentheses; this is an interactive process.

It'll start out as one thing and end up looking like another as different elements are added, experimented with, and discarded (until you think it might be worth trying again with different combinations). Sometimes it'll be like walking through molasses, or walking backwards. It might feel as if you are always hustling and getting nowhere. Success is tricky, but it's not as tricky as it's made out to be; people often overcomplicate things to justify their fees.

What's the point of this? Talk to your peers and colleagues so you can discuss the merits of these approaches. Find your own way. I want you to build something that lasts, so that you'll never have to say, 'If I had known then what I know now....'

Together, we will work towards a favourable outcome. We're supposed to help each other. For one person to succeed, another person doesn't have to fail. Another's failure won't change what you have to do next. Hope for the best, but by all means plan for the worst. You'll be somewhere in between. The aim is to get you as far along as fast as possible.

It's strange that particle physicists can write the rules that govern the entire known universe with a few simple equations. (Once you can prove something, repeatedly and by observation and experimentation, it becomes second nature – simple). Cricket, on the other hand, has a very big book of laws, and who can predict the outcome of a game of cricket? There are so many variables, any of which can affect the outcome. The same is true with your business.

Thinking Allowed is a how-to guide. It is not intended to be detailed analysis; it is merely a collection of tips and hints from business books, Internet gurus, colleagues, co-workers, and clients. We'll explore buyers' behaviours, relationships, CET-accredited presentations, and thirty years of projects in a fantastic business. There is no right or wrong way to build your business; what works for you is what is important.

If you read nothing else apart from this, please find a copy of *The Art of War*, first written on bamboo four thousand years ago by Sun Tzu. His words are as relevant today as they were then. It's only thirteen chapters long, and it's less expensive than a place at Harvard Business School, where its underlying principles are still taught today.

There are no chapter numbers in this book, just a menu from which to pick. You can choose to start in the front and work forwards, start at the back and work backwards, or simply open at a page and flick through. Whichever approach you choose you won't lose anything. There are ten underlying principles underpinning the whole ethos, so if you start there, the rest will fall into place. 'It's all in the mind' is also a good place to head next. When you find yourself disagreeing with what you're reading, return to the ten principles for the context. If you still disagree, you are still right.

Your ideas of better and success will be different from someone else's. As a result, your business is almost certainly in a different place than that of your competitors. Let's look at everything so we can give you a snapshot. You'll find the only metric we refer to is the one few people actually measure: happiness.

The best time to consult a map is before you start your journey. Sometimes you have to stop, take a look around, get your bearings, reassess your situation, and look at the signposts. Hope and despair will not be destinations for you. Think of it this way: can you make rapid progress by constantly looking in the rear-view mirror? Is that a sensible way to drive forwards? The road travelled is not necessarily a good guide as to what lies around the next corner.

Each brief menu item can be read in isolation and in any order. Each will end with you making a few decisions: to do or not to do, and how to do it (or not to do it).

Thinking Allowed aims to create a framework within which you can tell your own story. After all, who has the right to tell you to grow, to buy this and get that, or to do it their way? Our mantra is 'do it your way'. Who has a monopoly on the truth? What about the rules about choosing your ideal clients, dealing with the suppliers, paying the price you want to pay, and being rewarded with a price people are happy to pay? If you can do all this, then you will be able to chart your own course. The seas may get a little rough, and there are wreckers who will haunt your every moment. If the ship is sound and the captain and crew are well trained, well drilled, and well briefed, then you'll be okay. Most sailors know the waters will get stormy, but they still go to sea.

We all have the same resources with which to function: twenty-six letters, twenty-four hours, seven days, and one brain (arguably the most complex thing in the known universe). We choose to spend 30 per cent of our waking hours over forty years working in optics. That time is the biggest investment you might ever make. Forget the house and car – the first aim in business is not to lose money.

We all make thousands of choices each day: which book to read, which website to visit, or which type of food to eat for lunch. You can't read all the books, surf the entire Internet, or spend a lot of time trying to get all the decisions right. If you did, there would be no time to do the important work. The aim of *Thinking Allowed* is to help you maximise your professional and clinical skills so you can make the very best of everything you've got. Leave nothing to chance. Exercise free will – and if you choose not to, you have still made a choice. Everything you do has implications for the business. To get the most out of *Thinking Allowed*, you may have to read the whole book twice, or even three times. As all the performance coaches tell their elite athletes, it's in the margins that the race is won or lost.

Do you think your business is stuck? E-mail jwiles@blueyonder.co.uk for personal advice. Please put '86 Questions' in the subject line, and you'll be on your way to unsticking it. Then you'll be ready to come back and read *Thinking Allowed* with a renewed purpose.

If you like to make notes, don't. Most themes end with some suggestions as to the next steps to building a better optical business. If you want the business health check, the initial report is free. Any subsequent professional consultations with the relevant professional will involve an investment in your business.

If you are looking for a quick fix, a magic bullet, or a cast-iron guarantee that this'll work, then I'll save you the disappointment: Put the book down, and go do something else instead. If you are looking for a 'do this, get that' process, you won't find it here. That's what they taught you at university – and you believed them. (That's why you are reading this, isn't it?) There are no guarantees or reassurances, and there is no respite from doing the hard work. Sometimes time and chance helps a business, but sometimes they leave you unprepared. Sometimes it will be like walking through molasses, always doing something but seemingly going nowhere fast. After a frustrating day, you might find yourself thinking, *Is this how it is going to be, as it ought to be, or how it is?* If you are working hard towards a favourable outcome, then read on.

It's all about the solving, not the problems. Solving interesting problems could be worth hundreds of thousands of pounds over a thirty-year career, especially if you keep tinkering with them like a hobby. They'll never be finished because of time and money. But that is not a *problem* – it's a *hobby.* (And that's the point of a hobby, isn't it?)

It'll take time to get there, but if you stick to it, you will succeed. As the tools get easier, the thinking will get harder. Get used to it. You may be spellbound with the upward progression, and some of this may be beyond your comprehension or beyond what you dreamed possible. Remember that thinking too hard is as bad as not thinking at all.

Like most people, you will know a number of things for certain – facts and expert opinions that exist everywhere. But your facts are different from someone else's facts, which makes them fiction. That is why you must create your own narrative, your own story, and write your own destiny. Made-up stories are better than facts.

Solving the problems are relatively easy, but getting to the final destination isn't. Time, money, and inclination can waver occasionally. That's a frustratingly natural progression – the law of unintended consequences coming back to bite you. 'We all know the plan. We all know how it works' is not a bad mantra because commerce is taking place all around you. 'Happy with the plan?' 'It's a great plan, boss.' That's a great way to think until something unexpected happens, and then you will have to improvise. Don't worry. Einstein, arguably the greatest thinker of the modern age, was wrong when describing the cosmological constant. Georges Lemaitre thought so, as did Alexander Friedman, and Edwin Hubble proved it using the concept of red shift. Light matters.

This is all about the elements. It's not an exact science; it's more like alchemy, but with a significant difference. You are familiar with the elements, and you know they are proven facts in almost all known successful business ventures. What doesn't work today might give better results under slightly different conditions. To those of you who think marketing doesn't work, you may be right, but ask yourself one question: 'What if it's the one thing that *does* work, if it's done well?' Can you afford to be so certain? The formula that works for you will be different from the formula that works for someone else because of the different personalities, the variable conditions, and the times and pressures involved. It's also crucial how quickly you learn from the results and act on your discoveries. It will be the difference that makes the difference.

If there is one thing you can be certain of, it's that you have everything you need, or at least you can get hold of it. Sometimes optimists win, like they deserve to.

This is a simple treatise built for how things are, not for how they should be. The real profits lie in long-term relationships and explain why you see the mad dash for increased footfall amongst the retailers, who would die for the time you can spend with your clients. The days of short-term profits are long gone. If people feel (or have been told) that they have been ripped off, you've lost them for good. Feelings are important, and feelings can be hurt.

But do you want to get better? It seems like a stupid question. Of course we want our businesses, our organizations, our work, and our health to improve. But often we don't take the steps to make it happen. Better means change, and change means risk, and risk means fear. The organization might be filled with people who have been punished when they try to make things better, and people are afraid. It's a familiar feeling to anyone who has been to the doctor and not finished the prescribed course. It's often easier to shrug than it is to care.

There are countless ways to listen, engage with users, learn, and improve, but before you or your organization waste time on any of them, first a question must be answered: 'Do we want to get better?'

Not quite sure what to expect? That's a good thing, because the game goes to the fastest thinker. That's all you need to be. Things rarely turn out the way you think they will. Being a little bit unconventional is the fourth of the four things you need to be. Be a smart and hard worker who pays attention and thinks laterally. Reasonable prudence is acceptable. Be sceptical by all means, but not too sceptical. Too much scepticism leads to paranoia and paralysis. Intuition should not be ignored. If you've ever wondered why you've wondered why, this is for you.

Just because everything is different, that doesn't mean anything has changed. We wish you well.

THE MENU

Ten Ways to Grow Your Business Profitably, Sustainably, and Ethically

There are probably more ways, and all of them are perfectly valid, but these are outside our scope: acquisition, refit, joint ventures or franchising, remodelling your business to separate out the clinical from the dispensing function, and relocation. The real profit killers are costs and expenditure, and they might be the easiest and quickest to address. Employing the right people is fundamental to your success. 'Hire for personality, train for brains' is probably the best advice around. Contracts of employment and shareholder agreements, if not written properly, could ruin an otherwise sound business if they are not watertight. Tax affairs are important, and there are specialists who can help you. This is part of your overall vision for the business, and only you can help you with that. There are whole books on each of these areas.

The most profitable area of all is to do everything you can to retain your existing clients. Most clients who leave your practice are probably satisfied with your products and services, but they have exercised their right to roam, to find 'something better', to choose something different. People leave for all sorts of perfectly valid reasons: they move, they die, their personal circumstances change, or they find somewhere more convenient, cheaper, or faster. It's important to discover why people buy from you, but it's crucial to understand why they *don't* buy from you. The only way to do that effectively is to ask them. You have their details.

If you have done all this, you are left with three elements with which we will concern ourselves.

- Get more out of those you already see.
- Get them to come back to you faster than they would have normally done so.
- Find more clients.

Before we get going, there are two things to understand. Most of the answers to the challenges you face will be found in your existing client database. Without doubt, it should be the most valuable asset in your business, especially with a planned, systematic, and strategic approach backed by a sound information, communication, and education strategy (ICE). You will add real value if and when you choose to sell your business. Has your accountant told you that?

Second, you need to know the two most important numbers in your business: the cost of finding a new client, and the lifetime value of that client. If you knew it costs £10 to find a new client, and that client stayed with you over twenty years and spent £250 in each of their ten visits, how many times would you invest? If you don't know, find out now. It will change the way you think about everything.

Getting more out of those you see is a quick and easy option. Simply put your prices up by five or ten pounds per dispense, and calculate the net effect on your sales. Sure, you might lose some, but it's a safe bet is that most people won't notice, and the gains far outweigh the losses. Test it first. Try it on Monday and run it for a week. If it works, keep going until it doesn't work. Then stop and reassess. One practice I know increased prices by ten pounds per month, without any complaints. They stopped after month seven because they felt uncomfortable. However, the average dispensing value was much better than when they'd started. The right price for your products and services is what people are prepared to pay and must not be determined only by a formula.

Secondary pairs, multiple pairs, prescription sun wear, contact lenses, magnifiers, ready readers, enhanced readers, sports vision for active and passive participants, driving and vision, making lenses lighter, UV protection – the list is almost endless, and this program works well for clients with stable prescriptions. If for every one hundred examinations you carry out, you achieve sixty-five dispenses, it makes sense to develop a plan that explores the other products and services you can offer for the remaining thirty-five people. All the costs have been made in getting them through the door and into your chair. Letting them walk away with a cheery 'See you next time' is not a plan; it's a hope, and hope is not a sound footing on which to build your business.

Getting people to come back to you faster than they normally would have is not easy and takes time, skill, and persistence. There are plenty of things you can do to improve your positive outcomes: a formal referral system, a pre-appointment scheme, professionally crafted recall letters (not just some software program), a planned ICE strategy for the time between visits, newsletters, emails, social media, your website, open days, leaflet drops, newspaper advertising, and PR? Aligning your vision for eye health with what's going on in the community is a great way to stay in people's minds. You can employ or utilize experts in all these fields. Don't believe you can do it all effectively and efficiently by yourself? It's not weak to admit you need help. Again, each of these topics is a book, a course, or a membership fee in its own right, but some need not be as expensive as you think. Because you know the numbers, you can work out the return on your investment.

Local papers are crying out for interesting content, and by preparing a regular eye health press release, you can rely on the fact that the lazy journalist will print verbatim what you submit. They might want some advertising, but don't pay what's on the rate card.

Recall letters are still the most effective way to get people to return, and it might cost you more to write bad copy than it does to get professionally crafted letters written which reflect your level of professionalism. Are you still doubtful?

The direct mail business generates tens of millions every year. There is an art and a skill in doing it well. I'm not advocating a junk mail approach, but if you rely on recall letters to generate most of your income, then it makes senses to maximize the response to each letter. You have hundreds of skills. Who is best placed to tell the people whom you want to serve?

Finding more clients is important because you need to replace those people who move, die, or find something better (in this scenario, the only definition of better that matters is the client's). People's circumstances do change; you know that. Deciding not to replace them makes sense if they are high-maintenance or troublesome, or if you had too many to look after originally, or if you are deliberately winding your business down. But if they were good, regular, loyal people, then you have an issue that needs attention sooner rather than later. Do you know why people buy from you? Do you know why they don't? Find out now – ask them. If you are absolutely certain you are not losing clients, then you have no cause to worry. If you think you are losing clients, then you probably are. Doing nothing about it is a choice you make. Learning how to deal with it is also a choice.

It has been said that customers are like cats: no one owns them. If they are happier elsewhere, they'll go live elsewhere. Deregulation offered the people a choice, and they decided to shop around, because when people are faced with a choice, they decide based on the available evidence. It's not right or wrong; it's simply a choice, and you have to do everything in your power to make sure they pick you. Here's a simple exercise: write down five reasons why they should pick you. Do it now, and take no more than twenty seconds for all five answers.

It's a safe bet that if you did the list, it took longer than twenty seconds. But if you don't know, how do you expect your employees to know – and how do you expect the people who pay you to know? That's how quickly rational people decide, and we'll look at that process later.

You now know the lifetime value of the customer and how much it costs to find them. You know that half your advertising doesn't work, but you are not sure which half. You know that at the beginning of the new millennium, if you were told that you could talk to thousands of potential clients in your area for free, you wouldn't have believed them. You know there is no one better placed to tell your clients about your remarkable products and services than you, and you might owe it to your family and employees. The responsibility is enormous, but so is your freedom to choose which method suits you best.

Running a business is what you do; eye care is how you choose to do it. Providing a workable solution to a wide array of visual problems is important, relevant, and meaningful, because pretty everybody values sight. Tell people about your remarkable products and services, and let other people simply 'sell specs'.

The Next Steps to Building a Better Optical Business

Decide which of the ten growth
opportunities you want to follow.
Test a price increase.
Use pricing as a strategy.
Put systems in place to explore additional
revenue streams with stable prescriptions.
Create a formal recall strategy.
Find out why people buy from you.
Find out why they *don't* buy from you.
Look at all your recall letters and rewrite them (or
invest £295.00 and get 98 ready-made templates).
Find out the lifetime value of your clients.
Find out how much it costs to find new clients.
Evaluate your information, communication,
and education strategy.
Clean up and then look in detail at in your database.

Ten Fundamental Principles

- Trust your instincts and experience. Trust, knowledge, time, and skill are what make you remarkable.
- The market for what you believe in is infinite. Recommend smart products to smart people.
- Economics isn't fair, but chaos is.
- You work too hard in the business, and probably not hard enough on the business. Make it work for you rather than you working for it.
- Our perceptions are as important to us as reality.
- Reduce stress by controlling what you can control, and don't worry about what you can't control.
- Avoid working for a 'Splendide Mendax' company that thinks it knows better than you. Are you absolutely certain that their interests and yours are aligned?
- Think: Do you offer great products and services because you know about eye care? If so, you work for the brand. Or is it because you care about eye care that you offer remarkable products and services? If so, you work for yourself. Think about the cost implications of this.
- No one likes change, even if it's good.
- Change is the most difficult challenge, particularly for any second- or third-generation, privately owned business.
- It is through change that we can find fulfilment. Without change, don't be surprised if your results are similar.

The first ten elements underpin all the thinking here. The next eight are enshrined in your core competencies. They have been paraphrased elsewhere, but we will not stray from them. There is no checklist, but if you find yourself disagreeing with what you are reading, or you're saying, 'Yes, but that doesn't affect me,' come back and look at these pages again.

How to Buy Products Well That Will Generate Revenue for You

Ask yourself three important questions.

- Is the product or service you are considering a true technological development? Is it necessarily better?
- Is it a truly intelligent combination of existing technologies?
- Is it specifically targeted and marketed?

Why are these questions so significant? If you can't answer yes to one or more of them, then you have decided to buy a mass-market product. That is not an issue if that's where you are or where you want to be. It doesn't make it a bad product, but what it might mean is that your clients can't see the value in it and that lowers the cost of switching. Remember that your clients are making quick decisions, not necessarily rational ones, and somebody will always do it faster and cheaper than you.

If you can answer yes to all three questions, then you have a story to tell. It's your story, not somebody else's, which is something your competitor can't buy and cannot sell cheaper. It raises the cost of switching and adds value; price becomes less of an issue and may no longer be the deciding factor. You can now talk directly to the clients you want to talk to, in a way you are comfortable with, because you have looked in-depth at your client database.

You can also set your agenda and timing with your ICE strategy. You don't have to wait for the next cycle of reminders – you can talk directly to a specific audience. You may even be able to attract higher paying clients. Don't forget you do not need to appeal to thousands of people. It may be a more modest fifty or one hundred people, but with your formal referral strategy in place, who knows where it could go?

If you can't answer the questions for yourself, ask the company representatives. They should be able to tell you quickly, and if they can't, you can decide whether to buy it because you like them, because you need something, because you've always bought from them, or because you are happy to do so. After all, this is a people business and relationships are important.

The beauty of these questions lies in their simplicity and the fact you can ask them of any product or service.

The Next Steps to Building a Better Optical Business

- Do an audit of the products and services you currently offer by asking the three questions.
- Is the product or service you are considering a true technological development? Is it necessarily better?
- Is it a truly intelligent combination of existing technologies?
- Is it specifically targeted and marketed?
- Ask the questions (of yourself or of the person doing the selling) the next time you buy something.
- Pick one product or service that you offer, and discover if and why it is working for you.

A Fast Business Health Check for You

Here are twelve questions for you. Answer quickly and honestly, and remember there are no wrong answers. It's what you do with that information that is important. Doing nothing may be right for you, and if you are sure that competitors are not implementing new ideas, then nothing has changed. If your answers contain the word 'should', it's highly likely that it isn't working. Another exercise is to write down everything you don't know. It's scary but exciting.

- Is clinical and dispensing excellence enough in your world?
- Which is easier: create a new business, or reinvent an established one?
- How do I tell the right people about my remarkable products and services?
- In your opinion, what is the future of the brand? (Insert your chosen brand, or indeed your own brand, here.)
- What do you need to change?
- What do you want to change?
- What should you be doing more of?
- What should you start doing?
- How do you know that people are better informed after visiting your practice?
- Your market place is changing whether or not you like it. How is your practice adapting?
- Is your message interesting, important, and meaningful to the people who matter to you?
- Are you recommending smart products to smart people, or commodity products to the mass market?

Identifying the weakest link in a chain is important. Every practice has a chain, a sequence of events, and the same rule applies: Is the reception team briefed and involved? Clinicians will identify all possible visual conditions, but do they offer a possible lens for every condition? Is the dispensing lens led, or does the patient drive the dispensing option by selecting the frame first? (This has to be managed on a case by case basis, but anecdotal information suggests that lens-led dispensing generates more revenue and leads to happier clients, especially if there is an easy to understand lens dispensing aid nearby.) Do you practice ambush pricing, or do you have a menu? Would you ever eat in a restaurant that didn't have a menu and you'd had no idea what the final bill might be? Can the short-order cook working hard in a busy fast food restaurant change the menu, or does he merely serve what's expected? After all, selling to the next patient is easier than changing the culture – but easier isn't always the point.

The Joys of Freedom, of Fear, of Fairness, and of Failure

Thomas Edison replied to an enquiry about whether he had made his light bulb work. 'Not yet, but I've discovered ten thousand ways that don't work.' Most entrepreneurs rarely get it right first time, and there are usually a few failures along the way. The point is they were not afraid to fail, and having failed, they learned why and moved on as quickly as they could, with the next thing (hopefully) being a bit better.

If we didn't fall on our backsides when we were growing up, we'd never learned to have walked. If humankind remained scared of sabre-tooth tigers, we'd still be living in caves. To develop and improve is a natural human instinct. There are no guarantees that this thing might work, but we still do it, until we grow up. Watch small kids learn, and listen to the encouragement they get when they fall over or get it wrong. When did that stop? Why did it stop? When did we learn to become afraid to fail?

Freedom is frightening. When you have your decisions made for you (political dictatorships, childhood, retail, prison), being set free is troublesome for some, but not for everyone. You have to make decisions, think about the consequences, and take responsibility. When you grow up having been treated fairly and told that by doing this, you will get that, there is a massive disappointment when 'that' falls below expectations or doesn't happen at all. This brings with it tensions and anxieties, which are exactly the same as those experienced when freedom is your choice. You can do something about the latter. There is not much you can do about the former.

We have nothing to fear but fear itself, and fear is a weapon that can be used against you. Companies use fear to sell you stuff. They paint a worst-case scenario and sell you the solution. Extended warranty, anyone?

What is fair, anyway? Fairness is certainly a funny thing. It's is a mirage, perfectly visible from one perspective, but it often vanishes when viewed from another. There are at least three types of fairness.

- Proportionality: When output is linked proportionally to input.
- Equality: Everyone gets the same amount.
- Procedural: Honest, open, and impartial rules that say who gets what.

Strengths, Weaknesses, Opportunities, and Threats

If you haven't conducted a SWOT analysis, it is a great place to start in order to look at your business. It tells you what needs your attention, what you are doing well, and how you can develop. It should take you no more than fifteen minutes, and you can't get it wrong, but if you are not sure where to begin, you can find someone to trust enough to give you an honest answer.

Here is what a SWOT analysis might look like if you were a high street retailer.

> **Strengths:** Money, resources, people, expertise, infrastructure, footfall, location, convenience
>
> **Weaknesses:** Volume, consistency, lack of personality, limited range, communication, staff engagement, experience, competitive market
>
> **Opportunities:** Diversity, cost cutting, strategic partnerships, exclusive products, expansion (acquisition/new stores)
>
> **Threats:** Competitor activity, changes in the market, changes in legislation, complacency, red tape, heavy reliance on limited (commodity) products

Now, do the same exercise for your business and share the results at your next staff meeting. 'Oh, no. All our patients like the free parking' is hardly a ringing endorsement of your professional expertise, but it may be a real boost for finding new clients.

Patients, Punters, Customers, Clients … or People?

How you refer to the people whom you see every day is important. People are different and probably see themselves differently than you do. There are distinct personality traits; for every positive one, there is a negative one, and they all need to be approached differently if you are to make the most of every opportunity. You've all experienced the engineer who wants only the dispassionate facts, and the person who sees the world in more ways than simply precision. Both are seeking reassurance, a validation that they are making the right decision, but they want to hear it in terms that are important, relevant, and meaningful for them.

Patients tend to have specific visual needs. They are loyal and are maybe an excellent source of referrals, but are they your ideal clients? Can you make a living from them? They may not worry about what it costs to solve their problem, but it is also equally possible that their budget is under pressure. Two things are certain: they probably do not see themselves as ill, but they do rely on your professional skills and your duty of care.

The punter tends to be price conscious and will shop around for a deal. Punters also know what they want (or at least, they think they do), or they have a specific aim and generally identify themselves by asking, 'What's the price of (insert brand here)?' You generally have no control over why they came in, but the real skill is making sure that you are in full control of the relevant information with which they leave.

The customer may just be looking and making comparisons, but she may also have a specific aim. Customers are often price aware but may be not price driven. They often identify themselves by saying, 'Just looking.' Letting them 'just look' without engaging them in conversation may not be the best course of action for the long-term health of your business. There is every possibility that this is a one-off transaction, but if you offer a solution, who knows where it might lead?

The client tends to have a lifetime value to your business and may also be an excellent source of referrals. The ideal client (a person who needs your product or service, who can afford to invest at the level that supports your business, who understands the value that you offer, and who is a pleasure to work with) replies to your recall letter, keeps the appointment, and listens to and acts accordingly to your recommendations. It is a symbiotic relationship. You both need each other to survive.

Everybody brings joy into my life: some when they stay, and some when they go. People are like that and are very different. You can choose to deal with 'people like me' (after all, this is essentially a people business), or you can put a plan in place and train your colleagues to recognize these different personality types and act accordingly. You can choose to have a product migration mindset, where a people come in looking for one thing and happily leave with something entirely different. That takes a great deal of skill, training, and planning, but it may also be the start of a long-term relationship, and it is in the long term that the real profit lies.

You really only have to think about four kinds of people: prospective clients, clients, loyal clients, and former clients.

How would you treat the very first person who walked through your door? How would you act if the next person who walks through your door is going to be the very last person you ever see? Now how do you treat them? The last person you ever see, after a lifetime in the business, should be your choice and not theirs. It should be a happy choice because you made it, because you wanted to.

The Next Steps to Building a Better Optical Business

Analyse your data base and assign a description to all the people (by age, gender, income, pastimes, health, profession, etc.). At the next regular staff meeting, record how many people left without buying, and more important, why. The best way to do that is simply to ask them.

Remember, you have a 'stable Rx' plan in place. Train the reception team to recognize these signals. Describe and agree on who your ideal client is, and put everything in place to make it happen.

This will involve you developing a more sophisticated recall/newsletter/'thank you for calling today' program.

Don't judge a person on appearance alone. Devise a way with which you are comfortable, and migrate the people you choose to ideal client status. Remember that the profit today often lies in starting a long-term relationship. Remember that you rarely impulse buy. Are your ideal clients any different?

A friend walked in to a BMW dealership in Cheltenham. He was dressed down. The rep said there was no one free because they had a sales meeting. He went next door and paid seventy thousand pounds cash for a Jaguar.

YOUR VISION, YOUR PLAN, YOUR PEOPLE, AND THE PEOPLE

Your vision may be for a highly professional, ethical, clinically driven practice where chair time is fully valued and recognized by all. You may be happy to run a community-based practice, attending to the visual needs or the local population, or you may subscribe to the high-footfall, commodity-driven mass market. Or perhaps you will choose something completely different.

When you have that vision, you must comfortably do everything in your power to bring about that vision. Whatever your vision for the business is, be clear about it and make sure everyone understands what it is you want to achieve. If you don't know where you are headed, don't be surprised if others are not keen to follow your lead. What did they promise you when you started the course and graduated?

Businesses don't plan to fail, although they frequently fail to plan. 'Planning and preparation prevents poor performance' (the five Ps) is a well-known mantra. Starting a new business is often easier than reinventing an existing one.

It's never too late to formulate a new plan. A journey of a thousand miles begins with the first step, and version one is better than version none. There are no right answers, and asking the right questions is free. Asking your clients and your staff is one possible way. Conducting research (questionnaires) and walking along your high street to see what others do, are other possibilities. Having a sight test and buying eyewear from your competitor may be the most cost-effective investment you'll ever make in your business. Analyse your existing data base. Carry out a SWOT analysis. Look closely at the products you have selected and the reasons for doing so, and concentrate on the three ways to grow your business that we looked at elsewhere.

A good idea is a good idea regardless of where it comes from. Hiring for personality and training for brains is a simple guideline. The only reason for have a practice staffed by intelligent automata is if that's what you want – and more important, if that's what people want and are prepared to pay for. Auto-refractors are very accurate, but people still buy people where their health is concerned.

Everyone is involved in sales. People rarely forget their first impression, which is often made instantly – and if it's any less than people expect, it's entirely possible that your clinical expertise will make up for the shaky start, provided customers have not walked away. The best you can hope for in that situation is that they don't tell their friends. That is not the kind of referral you need.

Now that they are in your practice, you have to make the excitingly complex world of optics as simple as possible for people to understand. An interesting exercise is to imagine you are describing your job to a ten-year old. If the ten-year-old gets it quickly, you can be sure your clients will.

Offer plenty of choices (lens options, lifestyle options, contact lenses, enhanced readers, etc.) from a pre-selected menu. Put the people you see in charge of making a decision based on benefits, facts, and lifestyle. If they have some measure of control over the final result, they are more likely to be happier when they leave. Someone walking away from an optometrist with a prescription fulfilled might be happy, but you can bet that many people would rather not be on 'medication' in the first place.

Creating an environment in which people have privacy and time, which encourages people to browse, explore options, and ultimately buy, is not an easy task. But it is a challenge you have chosen to accept.

If people come in looking for something you don't have, what plans do you have to educate and inform when they are in the practice, or immediately after they leave? What would happen if you had a plan or a system in place to offer every stable prescription at least three things for customers to consider about their eye health before they left your practice?

The Next Steps to Building a Better Optical Business

- What is your vision for your business?
- Do you have the right people around you to make it happen?
- Do you have the right clients to make it happen?
- Do you have a system and protocols in place to help you with your vision?

What to Do if Your Business Is Stuck

It's very possible that you are actually doing nothing wrong, but is also possible that what worked for you in the past is not good enough today. That doesn't imply you've suddenly become worse, and it doesn't mean that things cannot improve. What changed, and why? How did your practice respond?

When faced with a threat, most animals choose between fight or flight. Some play dead until they think the threat has gone away. These are survival instincts that work. But what if the threat you face involves people drifting away, choosing a better environment, understanding a clear proposition, and finding solutions to their problems that fit within their budget? How many people did you examine five years ago? How many people did you examine last year? Which survival technique did you choose to adopt? Has it worked?

Here are nine ways in which your business might be stuck.

Losing out to the Competition

You are not necessarily recommending worse products. Do you need to reassess how you tell people about your remarkable products and services? If they can't hear you or don't understand what you are saying, you are in trouble. Are you sure the way you chose to run your business five years ago works today? Remember, if you are not working to make the competition obsolete, they may be working hard to do the same to you.

Innovate

Are you doing more of the same thing and expecting different results? Scientists would think you are mad. Copying what works may not sound like innovation, but it is if it's new to you, so try it.

You are familiar with the concept of differentiation, but being different is not much good to you if the people don't want it. Differentiating your service, your refit, the ambiance, your methods of informing, communication, and educating your ideal clients is a positive way of differentiation.

Not Selling Enough

Count the ways in which this can be improved. Do people understand your vision? Training, attitude, mindset, systems and processes, management software, poorly written recall letters, merchandising, lighting and better product selection, all play a small part in the overall picture.

Advertising

Bad advertising can involve poor (or non-existent) online presence, not seeing enough people, seeing the wrong people, and pricing. Maybe the old kind of people have gone, and maybe people don't have the time or the money, or they simply don't want what you offer. Maybe you are quoting a price people don't want to pay, so you don' have a market. If they don't have the time to listen to what you are saying, or they don't understand your message, then you are invisible. If they do listen and decide they don't want it, you are not going to get very far.

We live in a post-consumer consumption society, so you have to create a want. Remember that being a professional may not be enough. Isn't everyone? Many consumers are pre-programmed to look at new technologies, and it's fair to say that most lens materials are commoditized (price sensitive) and that most modern progressives are soft designs optimized for distance.

Erratic Business Volumes

Your challenge is strategic, systematic, and analytical. Maybe it's a failure of planning. December comes around every year, and you know you need a holiday, but you also know people go on holiday (and that your eyewear may cost as much as a holiday). It might help to begin the relationship as early as possible. Sow the seeds in the minds of your ideal clients that your products and services can be used all year round, not when you call. Why not align your year with the various health campaigns in your local area? What about the people who are simply looking for a pair of ready readers? Do you think varifocals are at the forefront of their mind, or do they have an immediate problem that needs a quick, easy, and fast solution? How easy is it to buy from you?

Check out your current clients, look at former clients, analyse the stable Rx/no sale, and study first-time clients (how did they find you?). These aspects are very different. They are not necessarily defined by demographics, and they may need a very different approach. A different strategy is required for each group, however you define them.

Two Real Profit Killers: Costs and Expenses

Are you absolutely certain there is nothing you can do about either? Review you suppliers annually and the expenses monthly. Act accordingly.

Pricing can be used as a strategy. You must keep an eye on margins, but applying one simple formula can lead to stovepipe thinking. 'I can't sell this because my clients won't pay the price' is a very different outcome than 'What if I could find some new clients who would buy this?'

Why tie yourself into a two- or three-year deal, unless short-term gain is your only aim? Once tied in, you have given up your autonomy and your freedom to price accordingly. Your new supply partner has determined your selling prices for the contract period, as well as your margin and your profitability. It may not be wrong, but think long and hard. What if your competitor refuses the same offer in favour of greater flexibility?

Setting Targets or Goals

Goals are anathema to some and natural for others. If you are not a natural goal setter, you have two choices: hope your competition is not setting goals, or learn to find what works for you. You must do what you are comfortable with. What might goals look like? Set short-term goals (carry out a SWOT analysis, ask some hard questions about your business), medium-term goals (review all suppliers and product offerings within the next twelve months, or clean up your database), and long-term goals ('We want to have a system in place that improves our examination-dispensing ratio by *x*'). The goals, the term, the implementation, and the monitoring of the results are ultimately your choice. The goals are whatever you want them to be.

Whether You Are Aware of It, You Do Have a Management Style

Simply put, do you micromanage or macro-manage? Do you work in the business or on the business? They are two different things. If the practice could run successfully without you, you have been working on the business. If it grinds to a halt because you don't turn up for one day, you are working in the business.

Don't forget that planning and preparation prevents poor performance. Change is happening all the time, and you can't control most of it, so it's important that you learn to master everything you can.

Your Business Has Been Marginalized by the Marketplace

You need to do something about this issue now. You can hope that your market share comes back to you, but it probably won't. This goes back to your vision for the business, because if you don't know what you want your business to be, don't be surprised if your clients, staff, and colleagues don't understand either.

It is also very likely that the eye examination and your products are first class, but that might not be enough. Who, then, has been educating your clients? Who is the best person to educate your clients? You must add value to the overall experience, and you must make your clients feel valued, special, and respected.

There is no quick fix here. The faint warning bells you may have been ignoring (for weeks, months, years?) may now be alarm bells. Too many people learn this the hard way – from an accountant who is always a year behind, or from a bank who says, 'No, we won't extend your overdraft again.' What is your distant early warning system and how does it work? More important, how do you react? Can you face the knowledge that the truth is not the truth, that it's obsolete or absolute? Getting rid of a delusion sometimes makes you wiser than getting hold of the truth.

Information, Communication, and Education

Information, communication, and education are at the heart of what you do. Learn to master every single aspect of ICE. It can be learned, and there are multi-million-pound businesses built on these skills alone. It is your job to tell the right people about your remarkable products and services.

I Can Do It

The can-do attitude can be a sign of weakness in some managers. It's like an orchestra conductor who may be able to play all the instruments, but the orchestral sound is much more popular, successful, and harmonious than a one-man band. Running a business is complex and time-consuming, and it may be that you can't afford to do it. It may also be true that you can't afford *not* to do it.

Together, we call all these factors Dorothy. Those who have read Frank L. Baum' s wonderful book *The Wizard of Oz,* or who were enchanted by the 1936 film of the same name, know that when Dorothy met the Tin Man, she didn't take him back to the workshop, scrap him, and redesign him from a blank sheet of paper. She merely applied a few carefully placed drops of oil, and gradually his years of being stuck were relieved painlessly and at a pace everyone was happy with.

Why might Dorothy be your most important member of staff? She will put you in control and get the business working for you. She will identify a list of things to do and give you multiple choices, and she will help you develop a systematic approach. Systems equal sustainability. Processes create a degree of predictability, and systems and processes together lead to profitability. They will add value to your business.

The Next Steps to Building a Better Optical Business

- From one to nine, prioritize the issues that most accurately reflect your needs.
- Identify what you are going to start doing and then do it.
- Identify what you are going to stop doing and then do it.
- Identify what you are going to continue doing and keep doing it.
- Identify what mechanisms you have in place for managing change.
- Draw up a workable timeline and start to implement your plans.

YOUR CULTURE AND YOUR PLAN

Your business has a culture, whether or not you know it. If it's part of your vision and what you want, that's great; you have a firm foundation on which to develop. If you find that the people you need to be with you are elsewhere, then you have a decision to make: re-educate them, ask them why, or replace them. A killer culture is better than a culture that kills. Everyone's business needs an organizing principle, so why not choose relentless forward motion as your motivation? Whatever lies ahead, don't be angry at yourself for being inflexible.

Changing the culture of a business is probably the single hardest thing you can do. It often takes a dynamic character to come in and shake things up, and the process often meets plenty of resistance along the way. Subtle changes are easier to implement, but they too may meet resistance. If you hear or think, 'That's not the way we do things around here,' then ask yourself, 'What if ...? Why not do ...?' Follow the theme, have a narrative with yourself, and ask you colleagues or staff for their views.

It is also worth remembering that you might not be the right person to manage the actual changes necessary for the good health of your business, your livelihood, your family, and the well-being of your clients. If you do, don't be afraid to 'fire yourself'. Recognizing this is not a sign of weakness, but a sign of strength. Your challenge is to hire the right person to do the job, either on a short-term contract or as a full-time role. They may be an outsider or a peer. Whoever they are and wherever they are found is unimportant – finding them is what matters. The phrase 'how you conduct your business' is something we referred to earlier. The concept of the enforcer is familiar to scholars of history, film buffs AND team captains.

WORDS

Powerful, positive, effective, efficient, productive, remarkable, memorable, relevant, meaningful, important, succinct, simple, understandable, thoughtful.

Negative, clichéd, irrelevant, uninspiring, thoughtless, careless, jargon, complex, impolite.

You get the picture. Twenty-six letters, three million words, and plenty of opportunities to get them wrong – but maybe only one opportunity to get them right. Words are important. You can choose the ones that work or the ones that don't. Or you can choose not to think about it.

Here is a quick tour of some words that resonated and were used by web designers – no doubt, to justify their outrageous fees.

Exciting

Claiming that something is exciting tells everybody that it's not. Instead, find something about your offering that actually excites the customer's interest.

Innovative

Did you ever hear Apple claim to be innovative? They simply are. That's true of every company that actually innovates. For them, it's normal, everyday behaviour. They don't have to point it out.

Sale

Your products and services do have a price, and maybe you've got some flexibility. But having a sale?

Guarantee

This is the word that people use to avoid – a word that has some real legal muscle, such as warrantee. Unless it is backed by the guarantee that enables you to give them your mobile number and say, 'Call me if you have a problem,' or, 'Call me if you didn't like what you saw.'

Authority

Self-aggrandizement is an unattractive trait. Unless it's in a written testimonial, the word carries little weight with those who matter.

Motivated

Never take credit for things you are supposed to do or supposed to be. Just do it. Actions often speak louder than words.

Dynamic

If you are 'vigorously active and forceful', um, stay away. Besides, you will frighten away those clients who are of a more gentle persuasion – which is okay if you want to.

Expert

If you refer to yourself that way, it's obvious you're trying too hard to impress other people – or yourself.

Passionate

Don't use this word. Try the words focus, concentration, or specialization instead.

Recall letters are probably the most powerful tool you have, and the skills of a professional copywriter must not be under estimated. After all, they are employed by retailers to attract your clients to buy stuff they want. There is a way you can double-check the effectiveness of a powerfully written and thoughtful recall letter.

Here are fifteen words that you should consider incorporating into all of your information, communication, and educational activities. The words you use to communicate with your clients are very important, whether in brochures, letters, advertisements, email, on websites, or in telephone and face-to-face conversations.

Easy

Everyone wants stuff that's easy. We want things to be easy to use, we want results to be easier to achieve – we want everything easy. If your product or service makes people's lives easier, make sure you tell them.

You

This is the magic word used in the most effective text. Using the word 'you' forces you to have a personal conversation with the person reading it. Don't you agree?

Now

There comes a point when you need to tell your customer what to do. They need to call you, or order from you, or 'click here'. But you don't want them doing it tomorrow or next week. You want them to do it now – so tell them.

Free

This word is very powerful. People love anything that's free. It's particularly useful to generate new clients (if you want to attract the type who don't want to pay for anything). But what about a free, simple-to-understand report about the importance of eye health and regular sight tests emailed immediately to their electronic device and accompanied by your phone number?

No Risk

Anything you can do to reduce the risk for your customers will increase your revenue. Your customers may not be consciously thinking about it, but subconsciously they're worrying about risking money (and possibly time) by doing business with you. Risk elimination is one of the most effective information, communication, and education strategies available to you.

Guaranteed/Warrantee

The ultimate risk elimination is the guarantee or warrantee. Adding this to advertisements for example will often increase response rates by 30 per cent or more. Test it.

Yes

There's something about the word yes that works wonders. When you speak to customers, use it a lot. It's equally important to avoid the word no.

Important

It's important to use the word 'important'. People want to know about important things, and it's a word that grabs their attention. And that's important!

Your Client's Name

In many contexts, the most important word you can use is the customer's name. The more personalised your recall letters are, the higher the response. Email auto-responders enable you to send hundreds or thousands of personalized messages at the same time.

Fast

We all want things to happen faster. If you can do it, tell them.

Proven/Proof

It's often useful to assume that people reading your message do not believe what you're telling them. It may not be the case for all of them, but it's likely that a good proportion is sceptical. Offer proof wherever you can.

New

Everyone wants the new thing. We may be bored with advertisements, but if they promise us something new, that can get our interest. 'What's new and what's different?' was a familiar greeting to a novice frame rep in the mid-1980s and it's still the same today.

Limited

If there is a genuine limit to what you are offering or the number of people who can have it, it's worth making a big deal about that. Scarcity is an important tool if you want to increase profitable and sustainable revenue.

Simple

People believe that their lives are very complicated, so anything that simplifies the process will have their attention.

Solve

One of the simplest copywriting formulas (the use of powerful words) is to state the customers' problem, tell them you can solve it, and then tell them precisely how you're going to solve it.

The next step: check all of your copy, both online and offline, and look for where you can add these revenue-generating words. It's even worth testing your current response rates against different copy using these words. Also be aware that in your own market, there will be other specific words not on this list to which your customers will respond.

Should

If ever you find yourself using this word, it often means that it (whatever it is) is not working. Patients should come back very two years. They should respond to your recall letters immediately. They should care about their eye health. They should spend a little more to get the very best they can afford. Suppliers should do a little more to support you. You should get around to doing a practice audit every year. You should be able to put your prices up regularly.

'Should' is an interesting word. You should think about its implications more often, and you should choose to act upon your findings. Your expensive education should result in all your recommendations being followed. But if all of the people who had received first-class eye care choose to buy their eyewear elsewhere, what use is 'should' to you?

The Next Steps to Building a Better Optical Business

- Check to see if any of the copy you use in any methods of communication can be rewritten or rephrased.
- Remember, the objective is to appeal to prospective clients, former clients, existing clients, and loyal clients.
- Consider using the services of a professional copywriter.
- Buy off-the-shelf recall letter templates. Don't use the ones that come free with PMS.
- Look at your competitor's website. What do you think?
- Now look at your website. What do you think?
- Don't under any circumstances let your web designer write the copy for your website.

CHANGE: WHAT WILL YOU START, STOP, OR CONTINUE?

Change challenges our behaviour, which makes it is one of the most difficult things you will face in your professional lives. Change may be necessary, desirable, difficult, or painful, but it may also be welcomed and much easier than you think. Our perceptions are as important to us as reality. Approximately 60 per cent of change implemented in business succeeds. That is to say, after twelve months, the changes made are still in effect.

Change happens and is an entirely natural phenomenon. Whether it is good or bad depends on the outcome and managed change is a skill that can be learned, adapted, and refined. How do you improve on that? First, accept that not everything you will do will be right first time. If you let that be your guiding principle and are not prepared to refine, improve, and try again, don't bother starting.

The process of change begins much earlier than you think. What kind of business is it that you have (or want), and what is your mission statement? Are your personal and professional goals clearly established, and do you have the will to change? What do you need to do, and what are the abilities, competencies, and skills of everyone involved? Too much change is not good; not enough could be fatal.

You will quite likely experience some or all of the following stages, and probably in this order. There is a timescale that may or may not be under your influence.

- Discovery
- Enthusiasm
- The rude awakening
- Doubt

- Second wind
- Achievement

For every phase, you must be prepared for the following responses from all those around you who are involved.

- Mourning
- Denial
- Anger
- Nostalgia
- Fear
- Negotiation
- Choice
- Adjustment
- Commitment

I must acknowledge the fascinating work of Abi Grute, FBDO (www.krauthammer.co.uk).

THE NEXT STEPS TO BUILDING A BETTER OPTICAL BUSINESS

- Identify the five biggest challenges you face today.
- What outcomes do you want to see?
- Identify what or who is preventing change – and do something about it.
- This is important: if the barrier to change is you, employ or appoint someone to do the job for you. It might just save your business.
- Remember that change might not be as difficult as you think.
- Would you rather be in charge of change, or have it forced upon you?
- Build planned changes into your company culture.
- Find partners who buy into or allow you to do your thing, rather than those who insist you do their thing (and that it is good for you).

USP: Differentiation or Remarkable Products?

Don't you find it strange that almost all of the marketing gurus use the same phrases, mantras, or chants to explain why you should pick them? USP stands for unique selling proposition (or point). Some say it has had its day, but look closely at the products you recommend: hard resin, mid or higher index SV, bifocals, PALs, CLs (87 per cent of which fall within +/6DS), some metal frames, some plastic frames, some rimless or semi-rimless frames, or maybe some designer sunspecs or sports specs. Now discover and explain what is remarkable about that. It's easy to say, but it's difficult to be unique, especially in a commoditized market place. However, it can be done.

Differentiation is another phrase you'll hear a lot about, but what does it really mean? You can take a walk along the high street and make a list of what your competitors are doing, and then do something different. It's a valid concept (aim for high end, low end, sports vision, children's vision, complex work, or low vision), and it might make you different, but if no one buys it (or wants it), where does that leave you?

How different would it be if you were to recommended remarkable products? Think about products that are not just good, not remarkable in a 'look at me' kind of way, but in a way that people remarked upon when they were at home or with friends. The products should actually drive new people into your business who are keen to spend their money with you. They should remind existing clients why they choose you in the first place; when they came to collect, they walked away with a wow factor. They should be remarkable in the sense that your products and services were somehow different. Those of you who have bought something in a high-end jeweller shop will know how they treat clients spending their money, with kid gloves. Contrast that with how you conduct your collections.

THE NEXT STEPS TO BUILDING A BETTER OPTICAL BUSINESS

- Think about all aspects of your clients' experience in your practice.
- Compare and contrast with your competitors.
- Remember that your competition is not just other opticians.
- How do you expect to be treated when you spend £175?
- Think of the Ps
    - Product
    - Pricing
    - Promotion
    - Positioning
    - Publicity
    - Packaging
    - Pass along (think of this as a glowing reference, the nice things you say about the product if you were there when they were talking to someone about what they have just bought from you)
    - Permission (referrals)

WIIFM? By Interacting With …

'What's in it for me?' This is not a complex idea and will be familiar with anyone who has tried to get a recalcitrant child to behave in a prescribed way. There is a little give and take until both sides are happy. The principle is the same, but we've all grown up, haven't we? Not really. Are your clients truly altruistic? Are you?

We have all experienced the following: 'I'll think about it?' Or, 'It's a bit expensive.' What that means is that people really don't see the value of what it is you are proposing. After all, the discussion up until now is about your price and their money, and you cannot blame consumers for understanding where the value in the proposition lies, can you? You exhibit exactly the same behaviour when you spend your money. Just because someone says you should do something, that doesn't mean you will.

Try this exercise with every product and service you offer. The result will be that you think about everything you buy – and more important, you think about what's in it for your ideal client. When you understand that, you can pass along that knowledge and thinking to all your employees, who will then pass along that information to your ideal client.

To discover the answers to the question 'What's in it for me?' you need to list at least five to ten benefits for your practice and for your clients. WIIFM is what lies behind the statement 'I'll think about it?' or 'It's a bit expensive'. It's the starting gun for you to get to work, not to stop work.

The next steps are a seemingly straightforward exercise, and whether you do them or someone else does them, it hardly matters, but it will help strengthen your recommendations. It works for any product or service you recommend, and it works on the basis that if you and your employees understand, your clients have a better chance of seeing the value of your proposition.

It's 'So what?' versus 'What if?' It's 'Why should I?' versus 'Why not?'

If you ever hear yourself saying, 'So what? Why should I?' That's okay if you really don't like the idea, the person, or the organization. But asking yourself later 'What if?' or 'Why not?' is an interesting exercise, and it might lead to all sorts of interesting possibilities and may even solve another problem for you. It frees up your thinking. The thing about common sense is that it isn't that common. You may discover the key that unlocks a whole host of opportunities. And guess what? It's free, easy, and quick.

What if your staff was able to recite by rote ten benefits (WIIFM) of your lens recommendation when the patient says, 'That's expensive'?

The Next Steps to Building a Better Optical Business

Choose any product or service you offer and list five to ten benefits for each of them by asking the following questions.

- By interacting with (product or service here), I get ...
- By interacting with (product or service here), my ideal client gets ...

Five Essential Steps for Each Product or Service You Have

Buying your products and developing the range of services you have is far more complex than it was in the past. After all, you need to offer an eye examination and recommend the very best solution for the visual needs of a particular client, and people don't buy from you because you are a professional. The only people who believe that are qualified opticians. Once upon a time, you qualified, went into private practice, and after a few years bought into a partnership (or moved on to do it for yourself). For some, the security of a retail employer and a nine-to-five existence suited the personal needs. Now, fewer opportunities exist in the privately owned sector, and the going is certainly tougher than in the halcyon days. The world has changed, and so you need new skills to survive in the new environment. Tried and tested can become tried and failed. No one voted for that, but it happened anyway.

There is more of everything, and we are seeing the death of some brands and the rise of new ones. Technology is impacting our world, and the Internet has revolutionized how we communicate. We live in a post-consumer consumerist society, and recommending what people need is a zero-sum game. We need to be providing what people want; that is what they'll pay for, and what they'll come back for.

There are all sorts of criteria by which you can buy products and services: recommendation, what worked in the past, price, because you like the people involved, because it's always been done that way, because that's what your clients want, because it's a fashionable brand. There is a template that you can implement and follow, and that can be applied to any product or service. It is a discipline, and once you're familiar with it, it's relatively simple to live with.

The Next Steps to Building a Better Optical Business

If you run through this simple checklist as a systematic way of buying in products or services, you will instil a discipline that will become part of a formal system.

1) Product
    - o What is it, and why are you investing in it?
2) By interacting with ...
    - o Identify the ten benefits for your business and your client.
3) Positioning
    - o What price point? How does it fit with what you already offer? What are the features and benefits?
4) Target Market
    - o Who is your ideal client? How does this serve your ultimate aims?
5) Communication, Support, and Education
    - o Is the product well targeted and marketed? Is it supported with training and education?
    - o Are there e-learning opportunities or website resources? Has it won awards?
    - o What sales aids are there that are different?

Leadership: Personal Strengths You Will Find Helpful

There are some characteristics common to successful people who build and run their own businesses. You can read all the management books you want – certainly recommend you read one or two – but here's what they all have in common.

- Talk is cheap. It's execution that will set you apart.
- Launch fast, fail fast, and iterate faster.
- Numbers rule! But don't be afraid to use your intuition.
- Build a business with a killer culture, not a culture that kills.
- Pick your battles.

Serious Time Management

Are you untroubled by overflowing inboxes, unhurried by overscheduled calendars, not distracted by ever-growing to-do lists, and always having time for the task to be done? You are sharply focused on the issue under consideration and on the needs of the team around you.

Prioritization

Being highly and resolutely focused on the right issues is crucial. Triage nurses prioritize many demands and always ensure they spend their limited time on those issues that are central to the well-being of the patient. You can do the same.

With one eye on the microscope and one eye on the telescope, you can prevent a faint warning signal from becoming an alarm bell.

Crisis Management

Bad things happen to good people all the time, and economics isn't fair. But if you have a good vision of what you want your business to be, do what the island nation of seafarers has always done: batten down the hatches and ride out the storm.

Have you ever watched someone throw a stone into a millpond, and you watched the chaos turn into ripples and eventually return to its normal calm and serene state?

Delegation

Successful people are acutely aware of their own limitations and driven by the knowledge that they can't possibly do everything they're asked; they entrust tasks to others not by exception, but by default. 'I try only to do, what only I can do.'

Whether your ambition is to be a mentor or role model or to leave a legacy, doing so is surprisingly straightforward. Fostering and mastering these nine seemingly mundane skills which any good leader can learn to combine will transform any practice. If you can identify all of these negative traits in one person, it may be time to change jobs, but people may see some of these characteristics as being a part of any successful person's make-up.

The Ego-Tripper. A boss who is arrogant, shows off at any opportunity, and is in constant need of boosting their ego.

The Coward. A boss who takes on no accountability and often hides behind others.

The Micromanager. A boss who believes they know how others should do their job, who can't trust people to get on with their jobs and who micromanages everything they do.

The Incapable. A boss who has been promoted beyond their capability, has no clue how to do the job, and has lost respect.

The Over-friendly Mate. A boss who inappropriately wants to be your best mate.

The Bad Communicator. A boss who is unable of communicating anything effectively.

The Plagiarizer. A boss who takes credit for other people's work or ideas and passes it off as their own.

The Negative. A boss who can't say anything positive and instead turns everything into doom-and-gloom.

The Egocentric. A boss who doesn't care about the employees and is not interested in helping, coaching, and developing anyone else but themselves.

The Criticizer. A boss who is quick to criticise mistakes others make and is unable to provide constructive feedback.

AUTONOMY AND WHAT IT REALLY MEANS FOR YOU

No one has a divine right to the business, whether they have fought hard for it, lucked into it, or worked to inherit it. Leaving university or college cultivated choices for you: private practice, retail, career progression, or an opportunity to follow up on new experiences.

For those of you who have chosen the privately owned (independent) route, this is for you. Why? Think about the reasons you chose private over nine-to-five retail. Write them down and never, ever forget them. You now have the basis for your vision of your business. It's a world in which there is a huge amount to think about, a world of hundreds of priorities, and in which brands will play a part. Remember, you are in control of the part they play; they must work for you, and if their values and strategy is not aligned with yours, forget them. One retailer became the brand and did so without using another brand.

You deal with whom you want, when you want, at a price you are happy to pay and happy to sell at (and at which people are happy to pay), and on your terms. It's a relatively simple checklist. If you are already there, how are you doing? If you started out along the independent route and now find yourself inextricably linked to a brand, and if you are happy about it that's good news, but if you are not happy, where (and when and why) did it happen? Never forget that what is good for the brand may not be good for you. Designer sunspecs attract buyers and thieves alike, and it soaks up your cash flow. Your accountant, your staff, and your insurance company may have something to say about that. The chances are that you sleepwalked into it, that you lost sight of your vision, that something changed along the way. If that something was under your control, and you let it happen anyway, whose fault is it?

The point is not to equate brand with bad – far from it. The point is to remind you that your brand is more important in the long run. Chances are you will be around a lot longer than the brand.

Ask yourself, 'What is my business actually about?' It's about change, about starting a new one or reinventing (or unsticking) an existing one. It's about getting people to where they want to be, and faster with you than someone else. It's about meeting their needs and creating their wants. It's about the experience. It's about leading a team and influencing those around you to behave in the way you are happy with. It's about not losing money.

The Next Steps to Building a Better Optical Business

Ask yourself four questions and listen to the answers.

- Is it because I am a great professional that I recommend remarkable products?
- Does recommending brands make me a great professional?
- Why should I work for the brand?
- What's in it for me?

There Are No Right Answers – Only the Right Questions

People sometimes turn to others to look for answers, and there are plenty of people online and in the real world who are queuing up to take your money in exchange for instant riches. What is right for one person falls on the deaf ears of another. What is true is that the difference between a self-help guide that works and one that doesn't is often down to implementation if all things are equal, which they rarely are. At the most basic level, you all have similar university education, and you see people with varying degrees of vision issues, but that is where the similarities end. The right answer for some (develop a website, do more advertising, employ more staff, etc.) is not necessarily the right answer for someone who has already done all that. Everyone's need, wants, and motivations are different. What is obvious to some is a revelation to others.

Maybe asking the right questions about yourself, your attitudes, your beliefs, your perception, and your vision for your business is the best way forward for you. It costs nothing other than a little time, and it may start you out on the right course or bring you back onto the right path. The great thing is there is no such thing as a wrong answer – it's just an answer. What you do with the learned information is important. Two people may give the same answer; one may do nothing with it, and the other may find the answer they need to make a difference. Another great thing about this exercise is that sometimes doing nothing is the right thing to do, or doing something is the right thing, but the timing is not right. There is a world of difference between a one's state of mind and one's mindset, and it is what asking the right questions will address. No one said it was easy.

The Next Steps to Building a Better Optical Business

For a free copy of our report, which asks you eighty-six questions about your business, go to www.buildabetteropticalbusiness.com. In return for your email address, you'll get a PDF. There's no charge and nothing to buy, no reps will call, and there are no terms and conditions. When it arrives, print it off or file it, but don't read any of the questions just yet.

First set aside fifteen to twenty minutes and avoid all interruptions. Make a cup of tea (or the hot beverage of your choice), find a flat surface and a pen and paper, and sit with the questions facing down. Turn your paper over and answer each question quickly, without deliberating over the answer or the implications. If you have to leave a question unanswered, do so and don't worry; simply move on to the next question. By the time you have finished your beverage, you will have answered the final question – and if your beverage has gone cold, you've taken too long.

What you have now is a snapshot of your state of mind. It's where you are today, and it's not wrong or right; it simply is. The unanswered questions are gaps in your knowledge; don't worry about that now. How much about optics did you know before you learned about it? The questions you've answered are a true reflection of your views. Again, they are not right or wrong – they just are.

What you have just created is a blueprint for your business, a plan, and a mindset. The order and pace at which you go about implementing what you have learned, or what you need to learn, is down to what is right for you.

Don't be afraid of what others might think. If you choose to overcome an irrational fear, all you have to do is replace it with a good habit. Learn to ask, 'Why not?' rather than, 'Why should I?' Ask, 'What if?' rather than, 'So what?' Make that a habit. It will transform the way you think about all sorts of things. This discipline may open up several kinds of opportunities for you. The best thing of all is that it is free. Learning to think like this may make you more money. It's a choice you can make now.

Brands: Relevant or Redefined?

There was a time before brands existed. Were people's visual needs fundamentally different then compared to now? Once we needed to read parchment by candlelight, and now we want to read an electronic device under artificial light. How has the existence of the brand helped with these basic needs? Not much, but they do however help with desire.

Perhaps we ought to rephrase the question and ask, 'Have brands outlived their usefulness?' Legal disputes between large retailers, mergers and acquisitions, designer sunglasses' 'end of season' sale, and designer brands are now widely available on the grey market. The impact of the Internet cannot be underestimated. It will be familiar to anyone who has a visitor in the practice asking, 'How much for (insert brand here)?' Ask your clients about brands. How many are really that bothered?

Brands are now being sold on price alone, which is not really the point of a designer brand name, and we have seen retailers grow without a single brand except their own and the evolution of the 'own brand' designer label.

There is of course the exception to the rule, because if you have clients coming in and asking for a brand by name, they're willing to pay the price you need, and they are the kinds of clients you want, then go for it. Remember that stocking a brand is good for the brand, and if your brand strategies are aligned, then there is little to worry about. But if your brand values are dissimilar, it may be good for the ego but not so good for your business.

There is a debate to be had around the question about brands outliving their usefulness. Perhaps more relevant is the question, 'Has the brand been redefined?' If you can replace your name with a logo and have the product or service immediately fixed in the minds of the consumer, then arguably you have made it to the top table. Likewise, if your name is the brand, no tag line is necessary.

The brand is increasingly less about the logo or the colour and much more about the process and the experience. How you interact with the brand, and how it informs and helps you, is becoming more important, and that is a great opportunity for you.

Your ideal clients may well be brand aware, but that is not the same thing as being brand driven, and understanding the importance of that distinction will impact your cash flow. Don't be afraid to build your own brand, which will be much more about the overall client experience than a logo, strap line, or sale. This will become your unique selling proposition and your defence against the dark arts of those who sell against you on price. It will raise the cost of switching and take you away from price sensitivity.

The Next Steps to Building a Better Optical Business

- Survey your own clients about brand awareness. Start out with lenses and frames, and include contact lenses if you choose.
- Instead of looking for a unique selling point (USP), ask yourself the question, 'By interacting with, I get …'
- Adopt 'a duty to inform' mindset based on your core competencies.
- Learn to identify all the visual needs and say, 'We have a solution for that.'

Information, Education, and Communication

Drivers, when was the last time you read the Highway Code? Everything you need to know about the rules and regulations of driving safely will be found there. It's much the same with the core competencies as defined by the GOC. 'We don't sell' and 'We don't like selling' are familiar mantras, and although that may be a true statement, it's hardly very useful for running your own business when your livelihood depends on people choosing to buy your products and services. Someone is choosing to pay for goods and services in return for your time knowledge, experience, and skills. The challenge facing you is to simply get picked when the customer has plenty of choice and no real knowledge of what's good and what's not.

Communicate effectively with colleagues and patients. Keep an accurate history. Have the ability to elicit issues: health, medication, work, sports, and lifestyle. Have the ability to understand patients' fears, anxieties, and concerns. Understand patients' expectations and aspirations, and manage them empathetically. These are phrases that appear in section one of the core competencies for ophthalmic and dispensing opticians.

Have the ability to appropriately interpret and respond to existing records. Have the ability to advise on and dispense the most suitable form of optical correction, taking into account durability, comfort, cosmetic appearance, and lifestyle. Prescribe and dispense spectacles for vocational use. These phrases will be found in sections two and four, concerning professional conduct and optical appliances. In other words, identify a problem and offer an ethical solution, which is the basic premise of all sales.

Who is best placed to inform your clients of your remarkable products and services? Who is best placed to communicate the benefits of the latest developments in technologies and eye health of your ideal clients? To whom would you rather the job of educating your clients fall?

The good news is that it has never been easier, more cost effective, or faster to communicate with your chosen audience. Thanks to the changes made possible by the Internet and technology, you now have the opportunity to speak regularly to the people you want. It does take time, money and skill to get it right, but once you have got your vision, your culture, your plans, and your mindset straight, the social media aspect of your business will fall into place. The Internet first came to prominence in the Western world during the mid-1990s, and who'd have guessed that you could regularly talk to people instantly and for free?

Is that marketing or communication? Is that informing or educating your ideal clients, or selling them something? Are you using your time, knowledge, and skill to influence them to pick you to solve their important, relevant, and meaningful needs? Thinking like a consumer will help formulate your plans. Think about how you buy. Do you always buy from the first person you meet? Or do you do a little research? Are you swayed by a testimonial or a recommendation? Have you ever been satisfied with the service or products from a business, but you've gone elsewhere for the follow-up, for no other reason than you forgot or it wasn't convenient? Perhaps the new deal was faster or cheaper, or the experience was definably better. Or maybe some form of information, communication or education reached you before you were due back at the first place. Who decides what your clients should read next?

Maybe there is a period of relationship building that precedes the first purchase. How does that happen in your business? It's true that you never knew your best friend before you met him or her. Most consumers need to hear a message at least three to five times before they register it, let alone act upon it. When they do act (visit your website, call by phone, or walk through the door), you must be in total control of the message they receive, and that message must be easy to understand and reassuring.

THE NEXT STEPS TO BUILDING A BETTER OPTICAL BUSINESS

- Audit all existing methods of communication and ask yourself, 'Is the very best that can be done?'
- Find out what works and what doesn't. Stop doing what doesn't, and spend more on what does.
- If you advertise and don't know how effective it is, stop doing it and see what happens.
- Find out the values for two most important numbers in your business: the cost of finding a new client and the lifetime value of that client. If you knew it cost £10 to find a client who spent £1,500 with you, how often would you spend £10?
- Critique your recall letter. Ask yourself, 'Is this really the very best that can be done?
- Critique your referral strategy and adopt a formal one.

Thinking
Allowed

Twelve More Health Check Questions

Elsewhere we talked about eighty-six questions that every business should ask itself (remember what we said about the word 'should'), which has some degree of relevance whether the business is brand-new or well established.

Maybe you need to make some minor changes or check things are going okay. Perhaps your business is not growing as you want or as you need it to. Perhaps there is an element of frustration and increased stress, or the future looks a little less certain. Sometimes you miss the weak signals, and all of a sudden the alarm bells sound; the fire started some time ago and smouldered for a while before causing panic, damage, evacuation, or disaster. It's easy enough to stamp on it and avert a potential catastrophe if you know about it early enough. Bad news early is good news. Discover all the things you don't know and then learn about them. Were you born with the skills you have now, or did you learn them?

The Next Steps to Building a Better Optical Business

- Write (or rewrite) the plan for your business and keep it.
- Do you have a vision for your business?
- Are your products and services aligned with your goals?
- How do you tell everyone about your products and services?
- Have you identified your ideal client?
- Do you have a strategy for converting a browser into a customer, and then a client?
- How easy is it for your clients, suppliers, and staff to complain?
- Have you got more (ideal) clients now than a year ago?
- Have you grown by significantly more than the rate of inflation?
- Are you examining more clients than a year ago?
- Is your exam-dispense ratio better than last year?
- Have you identified all the things you don't know (yet)?

Why People Might Not Buy From You

You can always blame the economy, put it down to bad luck, or explain that the competition is unfair. That may be true to some extent, but you have little control over those events. What you *can* control is much more important than what you can't.

It is more than likely that there are other factors involved, because it is unreasonable to assume that all your clients are satisfied and yet some still chose to go elsewhere. Perhaps satisfaction and being a good professional was not good enough? Perhaps you needed to exceed their expectations. Sure, some move away, passed, or simply forget about you, but that's life; you know that can happen, so don't be too surprised when it does. And don't be too surprised if knowing this and not doing anything about it causes you pain and worry today.

Here are twelve reasons why people might not choose to buy from you.

1. They don't know about you.
2. They don't understand you.
3. You're offering what you think they want, instead of what they really need.
4. Your offer isn't compelling.
5. They don't believe you.
6. You gave up too soon.
7. You don't have a clear, specific, tangible offer.
8. You didn't make it easy to say yes.
9. You've exhausted your list of contacts.
10. They don't trust you.
11. They're not paying attention to you.
12. You haven't given them a reason to act now.

The Next Steps to Building a Better Optical Business

You might need to consider:

- Appointing a business consultant
- Appointing a marketing specialist called Graham
- Appointing a qualified Dispensing Optician
- Enrolling on courses
- Hiring for personality and training for brains
- Using a formal training program (not necessarily CET) for key members of staff
- Subscribing to the many free online marketing gurus
- Visiting www.buildabetteropticalbusiness.com
- Emailing julian@wiles.biz

PRICING AND THE PSYCHOLOGY BEHIND WHY BUYERS BUY

This fascinating subject is crucial to your success. You can choose to leave the important decisions to your accountant or to the people who wrote your practice management software – neither of whom have to run your business on a day-to-day basis. They don't know or understand the complexities of the technologies available to you, but they do have a 'one size fits all' formula.

The easiest and fastest way to raise your prices is to simply do it now. Do you really believe your expertise is not worth an additional ten pounds per job? Two thousand five hundred dispenses later, you have just put twenty-five thousand pounds on your bottom line.

When your clients ask about price, they are thinking purely in terms of their money, which they want to protect. But what other question can they actually ask? You're the expert; they are not. You must think differently. Imagine they had said, 'I'm sorry, I don't see the value in that.' Now, how would you approach matters? Would you summarise all the benefits and ask which ones they wanted to give up?

There are three main issues around pricing: price pressure, discounting, and sales. The economy has changed dramatically, and that has changed buyer behaviour and perception of value for the foreseeable future. People are being more careful, and that impacts cash flow, which increases the pressure on any business.

Price cutting (e.g., end-of-season sales) and half-price second pairs may deliver a short-term boost, but in the long run it's difficult to get out of and it sets future expectations. That is not to say you cannot do promotional activity though.

Selling is actually about an exchange of value and a client who is willing to appreciate the value of what you do is more likely to spend more money. To do that successfully, you must set yourself apart from the commodity (mass) market, so you will need to tell them why you are worth more. People don't always buy on price alone. If they did, everybody would drive second-hand cars, shop in the cheapest supermarkets and retail shops, never eat out, and own phones that only made phone calls. It is a viable business model for some, but not for all.

Price elasticity is a concept you might need to explore further. You can set your prices in a number of ways, such as looking at the competition or follow a formula, or you can test your clients and see how much they are willing to pay. You might be pleasantly surprised with the last option. Try it.

Being considered a commodity makes life very difficult because other people set the agenda. But coffee is a commodity, hotels are a commodity, and airlines (to some extent) are a commodity. What's the difference? The experience. That is what people will pay for. Price elasticity is always there.

You could always change the products and services you offer—go upmarket, in the vernacular. But that is not an option for many, and for some it has proved disastrous. Offering a new product, something different, means that simple price comparison is more difficult. Scarcity has a value.

Why not offer a premium service above and beyond what you normally offer? You do have clients who will simply pay more if you treat them differently (i.e. perceivably better). Did you ever buy your mum the cheapest bunch of flowers? Did you ever buy yourself a premium or VIP package? Maybe you have 10 per cent of such clients already.

Introduce a payment plan. Bite-size payments are easier to swallow, and the more people you have on payment plans, the smoother your cash flow will be. One thousand clients sending you ten pounds a month makes life a lot easier.

A bundle of benefits is another possible option. Buy your polarized varifocals, and get the clear secondary pair for thirty pounds. Or get three hundred pounds' worth of goods for two hundred pounds.

Shirt shops will offer you four shirts for one hundred pounds even if you only went in for one or two.

What is the point of a free upgrade? Does it bring in new clients, or does it just bring in the same folks who were prepared to pay the full amount? Will it increase dispensing values? Does it actually bring in people quicker than they would have normally done so? Will they pay next time for the thing it was you upgraded them for last time, or will they wait for the next offer?

THE NEXT STEPS TO BUILDING A BETTER OPTICAL BUSINESS

- Ask yourself, 'How much am I worth?'
- Implement one or two strategies now, and test them.
- Don't be afraid, but do be careful.
- Think about the real value you bring to every interaction, and how you tell people about it.
- Don't listen to people who are struggling, unless you learn from their mistakes.
- Do listen to successful people.
- Take action and don't second-guess your clients or staff.

Thirty Possible Growth Areas

When you have a stable market, growing slightly each year with that growth comprising mainly of a sight test and with dispensing that is made up of prescriptions between plus and minus six, single vision, and bifocal and varifocal lenses, finding something remarkable is imperative. Growth in nature is natural. Growth in business is not. Uncontrolled growth is something you don't have to worry about. Planned growth is the only sustainable and realistic choice. Growth must be an integral part of your initial plan. No growth will be fatal.

Growth may be another word for change, for adaptability, for evolution. Survival of the fittest should perhaps be referred to as survival of the most adaptable. Might is rarely right, and big companies have a habit of collapsing as they lose sight of what originally drove them.

We live in a post-consumer consumerist society. Your database has a lot of people with a lot of wants. Your task is to find the people and what they want, and then show them ethically and persuasively that they need to pick you. Here are some possible options for you.

The Next Steps to Building a Better Optical Business

- Sports vision
- Active leisure wear
- Passive leisure wear
- Eye health conscious
- Actively link all clinical conditions to a lens recommendation, where possible
- Drivers' vision
- Children's vision
- Low vision
- Lenses helping those on photosensitive medication
- Lenses helping those who are naturally photosensitive
- New contact lens fits
- Rx sun wear for all existing contact lens wearers
- Polarised lenses for post op cataract and AMD patients
- First pair of Rx sun wear as part of an overall healthcare regime
- Trivex (protecting the remaining vision)
- Trivex and rimless or semi-rimless mounts
- High index
- Enhanced readers for computer users and mobile devices
- Blue light/UV/glare protection
- Digital lenses for single vision, bifocal, and progressives
- Digital lenses for complex prescriptions
- Reflection free coatings
- Hydrophobic and hydrophilic lenses
- Polarized lenses
- Photochromic technologies
- Polarised photochromic lenses
- Gradient polarised
- Selective absorption lenses
- Selective transmittance lenses
- Specialist tints and filters

ADDING VALUE AND RAISING THE COST OF SWITCHING

You can set your price low enough to keep people from switching, or create something unique that renders the other choices redundant. Raising the cost of switching is an underrated concept in optics. Once upon a time, we lived in a utopian world where the privately owned sector had 70 per cent of the doors and 70 per cent of total eye care spending. Retailers had always existed, but during the mid-eighties, a new kid appeared in the playground. What was it the new kid did that was so revolutionary? They changed the rules of the game. An easily understandable pricing structure, faster service, and a simple and no-frills offer combined with greater convenience. At the same time, they offered the early adopters a chance to learn new skills necessary for this concept to work. People reaped the rewards for their efforts by combing their newly acquired skills with their existing ones. Then they did something even more outrageous: they told people about their vision for affordable eye care. The message was important, relevant, and meaningful for those who heard it, and those numbers were significant enough to make an impact. Sure, there was advertising (crude at first), but after employing skilled practitioners of the art and rigorous testing and investment, it became slick and memorable. Branding was driven by an aggressive plan. There were also referrals.

Which was the single most important factor? One very likely possibility is that the cost of switching was perceived to be very low by those who switched. There was no risk involved, was there? The actual eye examination was the same, wasn't it? But the reward of 'significant' savings on a pair of glasses was a greater attraction than the fear of losing the service they had previously enjoyed. They did not see or appreciate the value in what was currently on offer. Some did later, when they came back and learned what we all know:

you rarely miss what you've got until it's gone. Perhaps we'll never know the real reason, but with all these new parts working together, a new business model was created. Guess what? You have exactly the same tools available to you, if you chose to use them.

Today, the Internet and aggressive retailers are also in the playground, and neither will go away until their business model is no longer viable. Then you won't see them for dust. Economics isn't fair. No one voted for the marketplace as it is now, but we've got it anyway. Meanwhile, the educational establishments and political bodies are organizing things for a world that they don't yet understand has changed.

Today people have over nine thousand doors to choose from, and millions of pounds' worth of messages to pay attention to (or not; it's their choice). Alternatively, people are a few clicks away from getting what they want. What could be better? That's where you come in. You do not have to appeal to the mass market – that's someone else's job. The only thing you have to do is make sure enough of the right people pay attention to your voice, believe in your vision, and experience remarkable products and services. Sure, the eye examination is an important part of that experience, but so is everything else you do (or don't do). The market for what you believe in is effectively infinite. If everyone on your database phoned for an appointment next Monday, what would be the impact on your business?

Where else can you get personal healthcare from university educated professionals and walk away with bespoke products, in exchange for a relatively modest outlay? Your challenge is not to be a great eye care professional; that is expected, and it is the minimum requirement from those who chose you. Your challenge is to find enough people to make your time, effort, and skills worth it. It's why it's called self-worth.

The value of the product or services that you offer lies in your clients' mind. If they don't see it, you haven't explained it in a way they understand it, appreciate it, and are prepared to pay for it.

Here's a thought. The next time you are looking for a receptionist, stop and think what the advert would look like if it read, 'We are looking for a Director of first impressions.'

All too often, we assume people know all about what we are recommending, but they don't. If people don't understand your recommendation, they are less likely to buy. Because we live with what we do all the time and think about it constantly, we presume that others do. As a result, we fail to mention things we know that are crucial, and without that information, people simply will not buy. The moral is to always show off your stuff to someone who knows nothing about it, and ask if the client understands. You'll be amazed what you can miss out on – or worse, ignore.

THE NEXT STEPS TO BUILDING A BETTER OPTICAL BUSINESS

Discover all the things you need to know about:

- Marketing
- Sales training
- Database analysis
- SWOT analysis
- Supplier audit
- Pricing
- Positioning
- Products
- Websites (don't let a website designer design yours)
- Social media
- Merchandising
- Advertising

The Scientific Method

You were trained in science, reason, tests, evidence, and careful diagnosis. You are smart, and you can solve problems by processing information and joining the dots. You have to hope that you are quicker at this than your peers in your area. Or you can work at it and hope they don't see what you see. Or you can hope that you are not too far behind their thinking. There is a difference here: they may not be working hard to put you out of business, but can you be sure? It's not always a given that for one practice to succeed, another must fail. Businesses do not plan to fail, but they often do fail to plan. Hope is a powerful force, but it's not an ideal strategy when you have a thousand tools at your disposal.

The scientific method is simple: observe, theorise, test the hypothesis, design a repeatable experiment, repeat again, peer review, and acceptance. Your chosen area of expertise is the visual sciences. It's not a stretch of the imagination to use the scientific method as part of your overall business thinking. When you deliberately employ the scientific method, you go beyond what you thought you and your business are capable of. In science, the simplest questions are often the most difficult to answer. Who? What? Why? When? Where? How?

By slavishly following instructions, you will never make anything new, but it is a great way for recreating what has already been done. Lego and Meccano is fun, for a short while. Scalextric starts off routinely enough, but then the racing, the track layout, and the undulations make it exciting and unpredictable. Flat pack furniture, on the other hand, has never been fun.

Almost every best-selling novel or record is a surprise. Who went to Steve Jobs and said, 'Here is what I want'? (And who'd have believed them, anyway?) The person who invented the car also invented the car crash. Chemistry, on the other hand, is always exciting, sometimes dangerous, often full of surprises, and always endlessly fascinating. Who knows what will happen next?

Science is largely an exercise in getting things wrong. Ask scientists what the answer is, and they'll probably admit they don't really know and need to discover more. Science is essentially about trying to understand things by a systematic process of failures.

The natural science of a seaside rock pool is an allegorical tale for us all. When the ebbing tide retreats, it leaves a trail of tidal pools, each a microscopic planet, a complete society. It's a simple mirror that allows us to reflect upon our own destiny. As busy little creatures living in our own world, we soon forget about the sea. Until, that is, the (economic) tide returns and wreaks havoc, and then new life begins again.

Great thinkers throughout the ages were mystified at first by the natural phenomena that surrounded them. They simply observed and thought about what they saw, or the effects of something they couldn't see.

Over time, they developed a theory, an explanation of what was happening. The logical consequence of the observation and the theory was to test the hypothesis. Doing this successfully required the development of an experiment, or series of experiments, which could safely test the theory and which would produce measurable results that could be analysed. These results were then compared with the actual observations, and if there were discrepancies, the tests could be repeated to find out what went wrong with the initial observation, the theory, or the test. If the results bore out the observations, the tests could be repeated to make sure. The final theory is then tested, critiqued, and discussed amongst the peer group until it passes into the text books. The interesting thing is that what once passed for as 'the truth' tends to be replaced by the 'new truth' as more research, better tools, fresh thinking, new perspectives, and reassessment reaches a new audience.

It's this process that lies at the heart of the information, communication, and education in our world of vision science. If you measure it, it will get done.

Behave like a baby because they are great mini scientists. They investigate, form theories, and test these against their reality. They learn all this through play and interaction, by doing and by acting after they've thought about it and decided on a course of action.

If the scientific method doesn't work for you, think about these alternative ways of thinking. The Socratic method has its limitations because some discussions elicit no truths implicitly known by all rational beings.

You could accept Pascal's Wager, which costs you nothing if you if you are wrong but might make you plenty if you are right. If communication (aka marketing) exists, there is a possibility if you believe in it and do it well, you will get your rewards. If not, what have you lost?

Zeno of Cittium was the founder of Stoicism, or the unquestioning acceptance of destinies. It's the passive acceptance of fate. 'Competition exists, and there is nothing I can do.'

THE NEXT STEPS TO BUILDING A BETTER OPTICAL BUSINESS

- Test a new copywritten recall letter.
- Test a series of copywritten follow-up recall letters.
- Test name badges in practice.
- Test staff training.
- Consider two-tier tests (GOS and a full sixty-minute exam with shiny new kit).
- Test a price rise: what would happen if you raised your test fee, a frame price, and a lens price by a total of £10 tomorrow? Fifty dispensings later, you'd have an additional £500.
- Test anything and everything as quickly as you can.
- Don't ever stop.
- Boldness has genius, magic, and power in it.

ADVERTISING

There are three kinds of adverts in the traditional print media, and it's hard to tell how well they work: it is not easily measured or tested, it is certainly not predictable, and it is usually expensive. The question is, how much can you throw at advertising, and which products do you want to choose?

If you know the cost of the advert and can find out how many new clients you get from running an ad, and you know the lifetime value to your business of that new client, then you are in business. Your advert might cost five hundred pounds, and maybe you saw ten new clients who will spend one thousand pounds during their next five visits. Your five-hundred-pound investment generated ten thousand pounds of new revenue. If only it were that simple!

The three types of advert are:

- Direct response: get someone to do something which ought to pay for itself; (e.g., Google, coupons)
- Trust ads: old-school ads, the results of which are generally immeasurable
- Demand enhanced ads: buy ice cream when the sun shines

Or you design an ad that does all three things. If you know how much the ad is going to cost and how much it is going to bring in, then do it or don't do it. This where the Internet and print media differ. You pay three times to run an ad in the print media (design, space, and frequency). You pay once on the Internet and you can run it a hundred times, change it, and monitor the results.

If you are going to run a print ad, then remember to negotiate hard. There's a rate sheet and the actual rate, and it's based on the people they reach per thousand. For small businesses, this is a fantasy figure. Start at 50 per cent with the promise that if it works, it will be for an agreed period of time. The reps work as a team and are target driven, so there is a deal to be done as the copy deadline approaches. Phone them a day before their deadline and have your finished ad ready to go. Because you pay for space, make sure the space works for you. You cannot get everything in an ad, so don't use a logo, graphics, or pictures – just get their attention, spike their interest, make them want it, and get them to act. Maybe direct them to your website, where you can tell the full story at no additional cost. The website may have a video clip, a free report, a full explanation, or a testimonial. The contact is all that's needed.

Social Media

For some, social media will be second nature; for others, it may be irrelevant or too late; for some; it could be a gold mine. It is whatever you want it to be. Websites, email, Facebook, LinkedIn, and Twitter are currently popular, but that won't always be the case. Whichever medium works, there are protocols rather than rules and regulations around each platform. For our purposes, these five platforms have some distinct advantages: immediate, relevant, fast, good reach, and targeted. If somebody had told you fifteen years ago you could talk to your clients when you want, as often as you want, and about whatever you want in the way you want it to be consumed, and that this could be done for free, you'd have looked at them as if they had two heads. There is one important proviso. You need your audiences 'permission', but once you have that, you have them. You can find out much more about permission marketing from Seth Godin, at www.sethgodin.com

As the tools get easier, the thinking gets harder. Each platform is separate and distinct, and each has its merits. What follows are just a few guidelines, some things to consider, and some things to avoid. Each subject is a book or a course in its own right, and in a world where you need all the advantages you can get, it's well worth discovering. Here are some general observations. They might be obvious, but you'd be surprised at how much money is wasted.

Don't try to be everywhere all at once.

The phrase 'jack of all trades, master of none' is true for social media as well. You have to think about what your ideal clients are doing and where they can be found. That's where you have to go first. Best advice? After your assessment, take on social media platforms one at a time, or not at all.

Think of social media as a college course: you can't take all the modules in one term.

Make sure your message matches the medium.

Here's a quick and simple guide that is easy to understand: See it all (Instagram), watch it all (Snapchat), know it all instantly (Twitter), read it all (Facebook), think about it all (LinkedIn), and educate them all for free (YouTube).

Is anyone out there?

There's no point to pinning your content on social media if your customer base is nowhere to be found on social networks. This is where your ideal client comes into play. If your ideal client is a single professional over forty who takes care of their health, there is bound to be a Facebook page that would appeal. If there isn't, why not create it? Who says you can't? Only you. Similarly, why post a discussion on LinkedIn if you're targeting clients who don't use LinkedIn? The sensible thing to do is pay attention and think about it.

The best way to get people interested in you is to be interested in them.

Sending your customers a survey asking how they spend their time and how they'd like to interact with your business is one way. Then you can engage them. Respond to their concerns, praises, and complaints. Can you think of a better way for you to form relationships with customers so you can better offer them what they're looking for? There is no point in running a survey and not responding to the findings. Do that and you lose trust and goodwill. Ask questions that allow you to make a change. If you don't, ask yourself, 'What am I doing this for?'

Always aim for perfection, but don't let perfection be the enemy of progress.

The perfect moment may never arrive, so stop waiting and start doing. Social media is just another way to speak with your loyal clients, former clients, and prospective clients. You wouldn't necessarily speak with these people in the same way, so that ought to be reflected in your social media content. There are no barriers to entry. Be authentic, don't be overly polished, and avoid jargon. If you can't say it simply on social media so a ten-year-old can understand it, don't say it at all.

Getting caught up in negativity is a realistic outcome.

Negative reviews and comments are inevitable. Although you can't control what customers say, you can take charge of how you and your company react. Negative feedback is also an opportunity to listen and learn. Don't get defensive. No business is perfect, so take a breath, stay calm, and get to the root of the problem.

Slowly fading away.

You started everything, and now it's being ignored. Ignorance is not bliss when it comes to social media. Revive, refresh, reinvent, or delete. You can't let things stay the way they are, so concentrate.

Websites

The biggest lie is 'Build a good website, and it will make you money'. It will certainly make the web designer money, but there is no guarantee that you will benefit. However, a professional presence is important. Here's a quick and easy exercise for you. Type in your practice name into your chosen search engine and see what happens. There is a whole science behind this, and it is changing rapidly. Learning from common mistakes your peers have made when designing their websites is the cheapest and most effective research you can do. Here are some of the most obvious ones. Avoiding these common errors could save you time and money.

Your website is like your practice.

This concept is not true. Although a practice refit is a good idea that almost always works, people do not primarily use the website to buy big stuff. They gather information, search for knowledge, and discover. Less than 1 per cent of people who visit a website buy anything. It may be that you have less than eight seconds to grab their attention, and it's provable that 50 per cent leave the site within that time frame. That is entirely different from your practice. Although your site is free, they may be scared you are going to sell them something. (The 'rip off Britain' mentality is pervasive and corrosive.)

So don't try to sell them something at first. Offer them a free (relevant), report which you send free of charge to their email address. Think of it like this: You are in practice, and someone drops by looking for a particular solution to a problem. A brief discussion ensues, and there is a light bulb moment. Nothing can be done just yet but will call back. A virtual interaction is just the same, but more immediate.

Think about the real purpose of your website.

Is it to inform, to sell stuff, or to solve an immediate problem and give you permission to begin a relationship (contact people later)? After all, the surfers do not know you, so why should they buy from you? Why not offer them something of value (a PDF report or video link) in return for their email addresses? You have to find a way to get them to stop surfing and do something.

Most websites scream, 'Here I am – give me your money.'

They should say, 'Thank you for being here. You must be interested in something I do.' Therefore you should add, 'You will get something of real value if you click this link or download this page now.' In return you deliver a free report or consultation, just like you would have if they'd explained a problem in your clinic.

Save money.

Many suppliers have websites and video clips you can link to, all of which will enhance the experience and cost you nothing. Video clips are becoming increasingly important, and the adage that a picture paints a thousand words is still true. You can even deliver that message yourself. If it works, why not? If you want to see what's available, go to some of these sites: www.drivewearlens.com, www.nupolar.com, www.youngertransitions.co.uk, www.trilogy.com, www.nupolar.eu.

Hyperlinks to existing Eye Health Alliance websites, NHS, and specialist sites are much more cost effective than rewriting entitlements. Remember to keep it simple.

Give an accurate brief to the website designer.

Otherwise, designers tell you what looks good. They may be right, but you want to achieve is something that works for you. 'Keep it simple' is always a good rule, by avoiding jargon and meaningless phrases. A simple test is to get a teenager to read it. If they can understand it, it works. Better still, get your ideal clients to read it. Listen to what they say. Avoid complex or flashy designs and a plethora of logos. The most effective websites are often the simplest (e.g., www.DuckDuckGo.com).

If the first thing that greets the surfer is all about you, then you'd better beware. They haven't surfed the net to find out about you; they have surfed the net to solve their immediate problem.

Bad text is easy to write.

Good copy is also easy to write when you know how. Guess what? The cost is the same. However, the cost to your business over a five-year period of missed opportunities may be immense. Bad copy identifies itself easily, especially if the text is historical or biographical. There are at least fifteen words that all successful copy contains: *Yes* and *limited* are missed out from the text below in this a dummy recall letter, which is offered as an example for you to think about. How would you make it better?

> Your vision is precious and important. Any problems you may be experiencing now are often easy and fast to solve, but some may need careful management over time. Many of our services are free for certain people. Call us now to find out if that's you: 01234 567890.
>
> Our professional training and ethical code of practice is your proof and guarantee that there are no risks involved. We'll explain the results of your eye examination in words with one syllable. Almost 40 per cent of our clients have no change in their vision, but if we do find something, we'll take our time with

> you so you fully understand many of the new options available to you. Call 01234 567890 now to make sure you get the appointment that best suits your schedule. Alternatively, email opticián@highstreet.co.uk

You rarely phone these people or visit them, so be very aware of the power of the words you use. Remember you are after a lifelong ideal client, and that your website may be a valuable (and cost-effective) tool for keeping in touch with them between visits. Do you have a notice board or news page? Do you have a shopping cart so they can get their contact lens solutions from you online?

Websites must not be developed in isolation.

Your website must form part of your ICE strategy. If you have an ideal client profile in mind, make sure that all your ICE strategies are centred around them. If you have a town full of retired executives who play golf, your ICE strategy will be very different from an urban, young client base. The golfer does not want to read about domiciliary visits when he visits your site, but he may want to buy a pair of intelligent, adaptive light, strong, protective, polarised, photochromic sunglasses at the click of a button.

Beware of prices!

You are not a comparison website, but if you are in a price-sensitive market, say something like, 'Our prices are market competitive, and our service is beyond what you'd expect.' Then deliver it.

The Next Steps to Building a Better Optical Business

- Speak with colleagues who have a website that works for them.
- Speak with colleagues who have a website, and it hasn't worked for them.
- Is there someone in your practice who has interesting ideas and an enthusiasm for this medium?
- Ask, 'How else can I reach existing, past, or potential clients faster and more efficiently?'

YOUR ENVIRONMENT AND YOUR PHILOSOPHY

There is no one right way to reach or define success. Sometimes it's found by non-traditional means. Here are eighteen secrets from lifestyle businesses that found success by stepping off the beaten path and doing something different.

- It is never too early to start. You don't have to know everything when you start a small business. Thanks to the Internet, you have unlimited resources at your fingertips, many of which are free.
- Hard work is good work. Dive into your passion, and believe that your hard work will eventually pay off.
- Define what success means to you, and then draw up a plan to achieve that success.
- A formal education will probably not be enough. Books and courses are important, but some lessons can only be learnt by doing.
- Persistence pays off. The road won't be smooth. Make sure you have a plan in place and goals to focus on to get you through the tough times.
- Risks are necessary. No small business begins without risk. The key is making sure that those risks are calculated, and that the returns are worth it.
- Be yourself. Use your unique skills and experiences to find a way to differentiate your business from the competition. It's worth remembering that you are competing for people's disposable income, and they might judge value not only from other optical outlets but from all other consumer interactions. Your one-hundred-fifty-pound specs may seem like good value to you, but that's irrelevant to a consumer who wants to spend three hundred pounds to look good and feel great.

- Consider your entire market. Make your products or services easily accessible to your most important clients.
- Try an experiment. Clients connect with *real* people. That's what makes reality television so popular. Build a business around your hobby or pastime. People buy people.
- Stick with what you're good at, and don't stray from your core offerings. They're what got you to where you are in the first place.
- Solve a common problem. The problem doesn't have to be complicated. The key is finding a creative, hassle-free way of solving it.
- Make life easier. If you can make life easier for someone, you'll make money. People are always looking for ways to make everyday tasks more manageable.
- Appeal to the particular. Not every practice appeals to large audiences, and neither do they have to. You don't need a huge market to succeed. Some of the most successful businesses are built on providing great value to niche markets.
- Try something new. Good ideas can become great ideas with the right tweak. No one has a monopoly on good ideas – and good ideas are good wherever they come from. Don't be afraid to copy what works.
- People like looking good. Make customers feel good about who they are. Recognize their individuality. People want to feel good about themselves, and you have no idea how much they are prepared to pay. Meet their wants rather than their clinical needs, if ethically possible.
- Simple is better. Not every business model has to be complicated. Products and services don't have to be overly complicated to be effective. Get the balance right between technology and personality.
- People like to win. Help clients reach to their goals.
- The little things matter. Some people may not understand why you're running your own business; they may not see the point. That shouldn't stop you

from being any less passionate about it. Keep striving for success.

- There is no one right way to run a business. There are sound principles, though. For some business, bucking the trend was the best thing that ever happened to them. Define your own meaning of success, and you'll be happier than if you are chasing someone else's meaning of success.

There are usually only two reasons success is out of reach. One is easy to fix; the other, not so much. If you're not achieving your goals and making yourself more successful, it's almost always because of something you either can't or won't do.

If you can't do something, maybe it's because you don't know what to do. The remedy here is to find somebody who has achieved something similar or identical to what you want to achieve, and to discover what steps that person took. Then you can build an action plan and execute it. Or maybe you lack the basic skills to do it. The remedy in this case is to get more education. We live in a world of almost unlimited information, so obtaining quality training has never been easier. Learn the basics, practice them, and make them part of your plan.

If you won't do something, maybe it's because you've got other priorities. Perhaps your personal life has gotten more demanding, or you're taking on too much. If so, you need to figure out when you'll find the time and energy to take action. If you don't find the time to do this, maybe it's possible that you don't really want to. By far the most common reason people do not achieve their full potential is that they simply don't want to succeed badly enough. Finding somebody to ask, learning the basic skills, and committing time and energy to take action takes a lot of courage, and that comes to different people at different times and as the result of different experiences. Maybe today is not your turn to step up; maybe it will be at some point in your future.

The underlying concept is that you can do anything, but maybe you can't do everything. The human spirit is capable of overcoming limitations and achieving goals far greater than one can possibly imagine. Whether you fulfil your potential is entirely up to you. Decide that you will succeed. That takes care of your 'won't' – all that's left is your can't. Fixing that may not be as difficult as you think.

RECALL LETTERS AND WRITING GREAT COPY

People buy when it suits them, not you, but unfortunately, you rarely know when that will be. You have to be in regular contact with them (once a week, once a month, as often as or more than the competition). You can't simply say, 'Our stuff is great,' even if it is, but neither should you always be sending them offers.

This is actually your most important challenge. As David Ogilvy observed, 'You can't save souls in an empty church.' So what do you do? One possible solution is to send your current clients, prospective clients, or lapsed clients an automated stream of interesting, quirky, and helpful information via your website. You offer people something of value in exchange for their email addresses.

Communications that your ideal clients want to open are the magic key that will help you build and strengthen your relationship with your audience. By establishing your position within the local community as the go-to expert for eye care, you can explain why they should choose you, and why you're better than all the rest. This will help boost your credibility and keep you firmly in their minds. When people are ready to enquire or buy, they are more likely to think of you.

Recall letters are the main generator of practice revenue, and under our existing business model, where the value of the appliance effectively subsidizes the eye examination, it makes sense to optimize the recall rate. You do the sums and think of the improvement in your business if more of your clients came back a little quicker and spent a little more. 'More patients more often' is an ideal worth working for.

Copywriting is a skill from which people make a comfortable living, and some industries pay millions in fees. They do so for a commercial reason, and some of the results are truly stunning. Imagine a scenario where you could send letters to your clients that have more impact and generate a better response. Letters that will not only produce more appointments, but they also strengthen your patient loyalty and lead to higher sales of spectacles and contact lenses. You want to provide them with the highest standards of eye care and personal service, together with quality eyewear that they'll want to choose.

You can do it yourself, or you can use the templates supplied by your practice management software, or you can do it professionally – which might be the singular most important thing you can do to build a better optical business. After all, who wants GPs giving advice on eye health? Going to a specialist makes sense. It's what you would expect your clients to do.

Most recall letters emphasize the benefits of regular eye examinations as part of an overall healthcare message, but it would seem that is not enough for some patients. You also have to pique their interest, inform and educate, differentiate your practice and service, be memorable and relevant, and get them to phone (or click) for an appointment. If you can do all that, it's likely more of your recommendations will result in your advice being followed.

The Next Steps to Building a Better Optical Business

- Take a very critical look at your existing recall letter.
- Take a purely analytical examination of your recall success rate.
- Ask yourself, 'Is this the very best I can do?'
- Now read your recall letter as if you were the recipient.
- Ask yourself, 'How else can I increase the recall response rate?'

YOUR FIVE BIGGEST CHALLENGES

If you are thinking of buying an existing business or opening a new one, you will have all sorts of challenges to overcome – none of which will need your optometric or dispensing skills. Turning an existing business around and changing its direction is often a more difficult task than opening a new one. Your ultimate challenges essentially remain the same.

Find new ideal clients.

This will be a never-ending project, an integral part of what you do every day, and it will be of massive value when you come to sell your business. People have a habit of dying, moving, forgetting, resisting everything but temptation, finding a faster or more cost-effective route to solving their immediate needs, or investing in what they want from elsewhere. All are very different behaviours with differing motivations.

One must not be averse to sacking customers or punters (prescription only) who simply want a deal or opt for the lowest common denominator. Over time, you will begin to change your client profile in a way that suits you. You cannot prevent against an economic disaster, but you can do everything you can to mitigate its effects.

Get more out of those you already see.

You have already taken the time, made the effort, and invested the money to get clients to take time out of their busy lives to visit you, so maximizing every interaction is only natural. No one likes being sold to, but people do appreciate the right advice, they like to talk about what's important to them, and they have come in for a reason. It's not a hard sell that's needed on the first encounter, but soft skills such as empathy, understanding, listening, suggesting, educating, and informing. How often do you buy on a first encounter?

Bring existing ideal clients back faster.

Use professional copywritten recall letters and regular communication of important, relevant, and meaningful information.

Un-stick your business

This topic is covered elsewhere in this guide.

Identify your profit killers and keep them restrained.

There are almost endless ways to stem the losses. You can actively minimize these elements, and all of them are more cost effective and often easier than finding new clients.

The Next Steps to Building a Better Optical Business

- Review and or formalize your referral strategy.
- Discover how much it costs to find a new client.
- Keep a record of how many new clients you register each week – and welcome them to your practice.
- Think of five ways to attract new clients, and act on each one over the next twelve months. Monitor the results and refine the most effective ones.
- If you don't know where to begin, email julian@wiles.biz with '86 questions' as the subject.

Things You Can Do to Build Your Business That Don't Cost Anything

Not everything you do needs to cost you money, and as such some things are worth considering. Making everything you can out of everything you've got makes sense, so try these ideas. What have you got to lose?

Test a price increase, even in a highly competitive environment. Reinforce that price increase with all the benefits associated with the product or service.

Phone your ideal clients and ask them what they need from you. Show them how you can deliver what they want. Essentially, it's free market research.

Network. Many towns and cities have business breakfast briefings. Who knows where they will lead?

Public speaking. Clubs and societies are always on the lookout for experts to deliver interesting subjects. Who is the eye care expert in your town? If it's not you, why isn't it?

If you are advertising and are not sure if it's working, stop it and see what happens. Costs and expenses are profit killers.

Public relations and press releases are effectively free adverts. You can write your own copy for the local newspapers, broadcast media, and magazines. Position yourself as the go-to expert for all eye care matters. You may be asked to advertise, but don't forget the rules about this.

Upselling is a horrible phrase and some may argue it's a dubious practice. But think of it this way: they have come into your practice to buy something, and they might buy something else if you were to recommend it. It's not for everyone, but it's worth a thought. If you can make it work, then everyone benefits.

If you don't train, you can't blame. You have plenty of skills to pass on. Put it in a formal context and make it a regular feature. If you can't do it, find someone who can. You have to hire for personality and train for brains. You must train your colleagues well enough so they want to leave, yet treat them well enough so they want to stay. 'What if I train them, and they leave?' you ask. What if you *don't* train them, and they stay?

Use email wisely. Turn the clock back to a time when you couldn't regularly talk to your clients. The only chance you had was every two years, or via a semi-regular newsletter, all of which cost money. Now think of the immediacy of an email and the messages you can convey – and best of all, it's free. There are rules that need to be observed, but don't ignore the potential. You can also hope that the competition chooses to think the same way you do, but don't be surprised if they are working hard to put you out of business.

INTUITION AND RISK EVALUATION

Intuition = Expertise + Experience

We rely on our brain to make conscious decisions and solve problems. But there is a thinking beneath our consciousness that we call intuition, and it is based on past experience or the very unscientific 'gut feeling'. It can't be proved right yet, but intuition may be an accurate guess, a kind of knowing without knowing how we know. It can pass too quickly for us to think about, or it might be a reflex action. The conscious brain is a bucket full of everything we know, and new information is compared with what we think we know. This new data is processed in the background, and once learned it's stored, to be activated when solving a difficult puzzle. You can call on your expert intuition (you are trained in the visual sciences, physical laws governing light, and the mathematics of optics), and you can call on the strategic intuition that is unique to you. Intuition can lead to conclusions because it is cheap and fast.

But here lies the key dilemma: it's inevitably a trade-off. It's where mistakes are made. Intuition is not flexible, it doesn't adapt well to change, and it can get you into trouble – but it can unleash the power of advanced thinking.

Ever wonder why some patients don't come back? You did everything right, but still they chose someone else for their future needs. Plenty of possible explanations exist: they forgot; it's not convenient; they remembered your recall letter but opted for a free test today, rather than making an appointment for an eye examination with you in two or three weeks' time; parking elsewhere was easier; you dropped the ball somehow; they saw no risk in changing (one eye test is much like another, isn't it?); all lenses are the same (plastic single vision, bifocals, and those 'expensive' variable lenses); there's an offer elsewhere, and money is tight; the risk evaluation (also known as the cost of switching) was negligible, the decision was made quickly, and no logical thought was applied.

Curiosity is hardwired into us; otherwise, we'd never have left the trees. But we did, and then we left the caves, then we left the land, and then we sailed the seas. (No, we had no idea where we were going.) The risk might not be as risky as we first thought. But curiosity cannot be equated with carelessness, and some people have a higher tolerance to risk.

Try this exercise. Which is low risk or high risk from these pairs: Shark or a cow, rollercoaster or a merry-go-round, bicycle or a pedestrian. The answer depends on you experience, circumstances, risk threshold, or best guess. Who do you think will be a bigger risk taker? The caffeine-fuelled adrenaline junkie, or the person who enjoys yoga and meditation? It will be no surprise to learn that the fast answers – shark, rollercoaster, and bicycle – are generated by the fast thinking that your brain does on your behalf. But in the light of new information and context, the other options are equally right. If you are crossing a field, the cow is far more dangerous than a shark. A pedestrian is in far more danger on the motorway than the bicycle on a cycle path.

Behaviours can be influenced and learned. You can train your clients. That is your challenge today and tomorrow. We are the most technical and rational creatures ever to have evolved on this planet, yet superstition still exercises control in some people, and it is not routed in science. Our brains have evolved to recognize patterns: it's got big teeth, smells funny, growls, and can be very quiet when it needs to be. Once we've seen a lioness, we tend to remember anything that looks similar is probably dangerous. Pattern recognition (like the lioness) is important. Pattern matching is for amateurs. The lions have fed and are sleeping; your passage is safer.

Innovation is not simple. You must make decisions without being able to reliably predict their effects on your client.

Decisions are made from a position of uncertainty. A gut feeling (or expert opinion) is central to making decisions from a position of uncertainty. This gut instinct or intuition draws on subconscious knowledge based on experience, coupled with the expertise acquired over the years.

The pleasure of seeing well and looking good might become the 'inspiring experience of healthy sight and looking good and seeing well' when it comes to pleasing your ideal clients.

Be aware that a large proportion of your experience and expertise may no longer be relevant to these future expectations, and that a gut feeling could take you in the wrong direction. (Nostalgia is not what it used to be.)

The Next Steps to Building a Better Optical Business

What are the options for training your gut feeling to meet the new challenges? How can your own experience be enhanced with material that is relevant to the problem? The answer might be to immerse yourself in the context of the future, by gathering relevant data and information and by identifying the future needs of spectacle wearers. It's a form of learned intuition. But sleeping on it may no longer be an option.

However you access this subconscious part of the brain (jogging, walking the dog, listening to music) is right and may also have positive side effects, such as less stress and greater satisfaction in your place of work.

How Your Brain Works: How You Really Make Decisions.

As a species, we like to think we are smart, wise, and rational, and that we make conscious decisions. There is plenty of interesting research to indicate that is mostly delusional, and that it's an internal battle – a 'mind field'. It's intuition versus logic.

Professor Daniel Kahneman is an economist and psychologist, and in 2002 he won the Nobel Memorial Prize in Economic Sciences (shared with Vernon L. Smith). He is professor emeritus of psychology and public affairs at Princeton University's Woodrow Wilson School. His central thesis is an insight into how we actually make decisions. Do we think logically, or are we driven by an urge to make a certain amount of money? If you are trying to maximize your income, you work very hard to fill the quieter days. With the diary full, you are happy (irrespective of what actually comes in). You effectively base your happiness on what's happened in the past. Your intuition may be taking you the wrong way.

Evaluating your mistakes is an interesting exercise. Are they random errors or a systematic bias? Most of our focus is on the powerful rational side of the brain and not the intuitive side. The human mind does not work like a computer, and intuition is a departure from the rules of logic. Some of the best clues come from when we get things wrong. Our attention is so limited that we often do not pay attention to what's in front of us – a form of 'unintentional blindness'. But knowing this still has no impact on our behaviour.

Fast Thinking versus Slow Thinking, and Why We Do What We Do

It's estimated we make between two thousand and ten thousand decisions a day. That's a decision every eight to forty-three seconds. Evolution has given the human brain two ways of thinking. The first way is fast –dramatic, automatic, powerful, and effortless. That's what happens most of the time. Automatic responses are usually based on visual perceptions or past experiences. It's always in gear and is ready to make a snap judgement.

$$2 + 2 = ?$$

The other way is slow – deliberate, rational, logical, the inner voice.

$$17 \times 24 = ?$$

When you pay attention (why do we use that phrase?) to a complex problem, you have to follow rules, and following a system with logic is slow and sequential. It's old and well developed. It's reason and rationalization. This involves work, concentration, and effort, and it is not automatic. It leads to physiological changes (palpitations, raised heartbeats, etc.). Interestingly, even being asked to do two relatively simple but totally unrelated tasks can throw us. For example, you can count in increments of seven, and you can walk backwards. Now, try counting down from one hundred in increments of seven whilst walking backwards. It's not so easy!

We like to think the slow system is the real us, the star of the show. In reality, it's not true. The 'real' you (logical and rational) is a bit part player who thinks it's the star. The same is true for your clients. The logical and rational thing to do is to come see you. People are often neither logical nor rational.

We have an instant opinion on most things – fast, intuitive, and powerful does most of the driving. It has to because we have lots of decisions to make. Slow, logical, clever, rational thinking is a little bit lazy. It's this battleground where mistakes are made.

What actually drives the decisions you make? The thoughtless creation of habits is something to be aware of, if not guarded against. Making a decision is often based on the decisions you have made in the past as if they were right (which they may have been then), but that may not be right today. The world around you changes, even if you don't.

Fast thinking accepts mistakes (cognitive bias) as a 'good' decision. It has a present bias focus. It's all about now, and we don't think about the future (e.g., texting and driving, exercising and smoking, unprotected sex). We know it's not good for us, but we do it anyway. Here are some other factors to guard against.

The halo effect. It is very powerful. If you like someone (in an organization, for example), you tend to think well of the organization as a whole, and vice-versa. (This is not always true if the rep has the brand that you want.) An attractive trait in an otherwise horrible person is difficult to compute. Adolf Hitler was a vegan who liked children and was kind to his mother. What we like is good, and what we dislike is bad.

The spotlight effect. This is where we think people pay attention to us. But do they really?

Confirmation bias. Where do your beliefs and opinions come from? If you are like most people, you probably like to believe that your beliefs are the result of years of experience and objective analysis of the information you have available. The reality is that all of us are susceptible to a tricky problem known as a confirmation bias. We like to imagine that our beliefs are rational, logical, and objective, but the fact is that our ideas are often based on paying attention to the information that upholds our ideas and ignoring the inconvenient truth. Confirmation bias is a type of cognitive bias that involves favouring information that confirms previously existing beliefs or biases. For example, imagine that a person holds a belief that left-handed people are more creative than right-handed people. Whenever this person encounters a person who is both left-handed and creative, he places greater importance on this 'evidence' supporting an already existing belief. This individual might even seek out 'proof' that further backs up this belief – while discounting examples that do not support this idea.

Confirmation biases impact how people gather information, but they also influence how people interpret and recall information. For example, people who support or oppose a particular issue will not only seek information that supports their beliefs, but they will also interpret news stories in a way that upholds their existing ideas, and they remember things in a way that also reinforces these attitudes.

Discuss the following statements: Marketing works. Change is good. My supplier is the best. I can do better. For those who don't believe, no proof is enough. For those who believe, no proof is necessary.

The 'key' effect. You like what you've created, and so do others. But do they?

Risk aversion. This is probably the most primeval of instincts, which has served us well. But here you have a conflict with confirmation bias: 'We've always done it this way.' Tried and tested may become invalid because the world changed, and you didn't.

Overconfidence. Just because you did it before in one set of surroundings, that doesn't mean you are guaranteed to succeed in new surroundings. Plenty of optometrists and dispensing opticians have left retail because they want to do it for themselves. Almost all never regret the decision, saying, 'I should have done it sooner. But almost all explain it was tougher than they imagined. They needed to learn different skills, and they needed to become different types of professionals.

There is often one way to do things right, and there are many ways for things to go wrong: trusting the wrong person, not understanding (or seeing) a point of view, impulse spending, post-purchase remorse, and resisting everything but temptation.

You have access to a huge amount of data, but you are time limited, especially if there is an emerging threat. Each piece of information is a piece of the puzzle, but where is the box top? Mistakes are easy to make. Experts are often the most prone to cognitive bias (economists anyone?). Most modern medicine is built on mistakes of the past, and when money enters the picture, the rules change.

We can all spot a bargain, and we all invest wisely, don't we? Cognitive bias plays havoc with our rational thoughts. If you gamble, how do you feel when you win or lose? Take the £10 winnings, but you have to flip a coin, and if you are right, you win another £5? Take the £20 winnings, but you have to flip a coin, and if you are wrong, you lose £5? Loss is painful, and loss aversion (where the losses loom larger than the gains) is a powerful driver.

The bedrock of our economic system is that 'experts' think and act rationally, but how often is the fast system used to make those decisions? Look at hedge fund managers versus Warren Buffet.

Assuming people make rational decisions gives us a problem. Optimism, overconfidence, and confirmation bias play large roles in our lives.

MISTAKES

The person who never made a mistake never did anything. Mistakes are part of being human and will lead to both good and bad outcomes. We are limited, irrational, and imperfect, but we can build something that works. The ability to recognize the familiar is important to our brains, and we trust the familiar. When confronted with the unfamiliar, it is the amygdala, our 'danger detector', that kicks in. It explains why we stay in bad jobs and bad relationships, and why we pay 30 per cent or more for brands. When confronted with conflicting information, we default to what we know, even if it might be wrong. Trust is a currency: it's reliable, consistent, and generous. Mistrust can lead us to miss beneficial opportunities.

Stress is part of our everyday lives and is essential to our survival; heightened senses and adrenalin are important for running away. But is it better to be safe than sorry? Is flight or fight the right answer? What about doing nothing as a survival strategy?

The Next Steps to Building a Better Optical Business

- Making mistakes is perfectly natural. Don't be afraid of changing (improving) things.
- What can you do about the mistakes you are making?
- Reflect. You have the ability to change
- People are loss averse. Never forget that.
- Provide a value comparison.
- Recognize that fear and anxiety are very different things.
- Fear can make things better.
- Anxiety: assess the threat as real or false.
- Use pressure wisely; it can crush, or it can create diamonds.

On Trust

Despite being a highly trusted profession, there is something irrational about the concept of trust. The obvious and rational equation is that being trustworthy, competent, and transparent will lead you to be trusted.

If that's true, how do we explain that brands like Coke and Google are trusted despite their ingredients and algorithms being kept secret?

Trust can be derived from recommendation or expectation. You book a restaurant without seeing the farm or the kitchen first. Trust is central to your success. Once broken, it's hard to regain, and it's hardwired into how we judge and are judged. What makes you trust a politician, a bank, a company, or an institution? And what would make you change your mind? Trust comes from the actions taken and expectations exceeded (not merely satisfied). Generally, people like us trust people like us.

Are you a trustworthy person or organization that fails to understand or take actions that lead to trust, and as a result you fail to make the impact you are capable of? Or have you realized that it's possible to be trusted without actually doing the hard work of being trustworthy?

COMMUNICATING EFFECTIVELY

Behaviour is learned, and it is the product of our genes, memories, thoughts, emotions, reasons, experiences, belief systems, and more. We can adapt, adopt, and change. Behaviours can be learned and manipulated (e.g., Pavlov's dogs, the Skinner Box, and countless other non-invasive animal experimental studies). The same is true for nations: people behave differently under capitalist and communist regimes, or under a theocracy.

Therefore it follows that you can change the behaviour of the people who are important to you. It might not be easy, quick, or simple, but it is important, relevant, and meaningful. Images and words, thoughts and deeds, actions and inactions, persistence and consistency, delayed gratification – all play their parts.

So, You Hate Selling?

Selling is a contentious word for most eye care professionals. It has unprofessional connotations for some, but not for all. But if people didn't buy, could your business survive? 'I don't sell' has been heard by countless reps. Until such time as the majority of our population wakes up in the morning with some form of ocular pathology or a highly developed sense of eye health awareness, and decides to book an appointment with you, those who do need eyewear have plenty of choices from where to buy.

The irony is that no one likes being sold to, but when we buy something important, we often do our research, seek opinions or otherwise educate ourselves. When we buy, we make smart choices. No one makes us do it. In a post-consumer consumerist society, it's important you get enough people to choose you. Likewise, the people who visit you listen to and act on your professional advice might follow your advice and buy a pair of specs. Is that selling, selling a service, or service? 'How can we serve you?' is much more likely to gain traction with people than 'What can we sell you?'

Your website is a great repository for your knowledge and personality to deliver the information and education in a way that is important, meaningful, and relevant. You believe in what you do, don't you? So do your competitors and they may already be effectively communicating their knowledge.

If you and your staff are good at building relationships, well connected in the locale, empathetic, knowledgeable, and good listeners, you'll sell a lot. Maybe your staff solve problems, make things happen, take responsibility, and engage with your vision. What do you think will be the outcome? These scenarios are everyone's dream team.

If you employ staff, it's worth remembering a few things: You got to where you are through a process of education and training, and you take pride in what you do. Your people are no different. Many people say, 'Training is expensive. What happens if we train them, and they leave?' Think about the alternative scenario: what happens to your business if you *don't* train them, and they stay? Good training is not a cost – it is an investment in your business for today and tomorrow.

School work (or more accurately, school life) is not for everyone. People develop at different speeds, and everybody's circumstances are different. People learn at different speeds and in different ways. Here are a few character traits that may be far more valuable to your business than academic qualifications – and they require zero talent: having a strong work ethic, being on time, effort, positive attitude, going the extra yard, being a self-starter, being prepared, and being open to new ideas and responsibilities.

Staff turnover is a fact of life: Here's a simple checklist that keeps this to a minimum: pay well, mentor them, challenge them, promote them (responsibilities), involve them, appreciate them, trust them, and empower them. These are not guarantees that good staff will stay, but they are the reasons good people leave jobs (and you might have to do more selling).

Another way to avoid selling is to think about how you can recession-proof your business. There is a big difference between macroeconomics (promoted widely and often negatively in the media) and microeconomics (or the local community), and there is very little you can do about either. Controlling what you can (by future-proofing) makes good business sense. You can control how your business responds to either micro or macro events. It's the difference between a mindset and a state of mind.

The Next Steps to Building a Better Optical Business

- Accept that sales are the ultimate growth leverage for most businesses.
- Make the choice to get good at it; face your fear.
- Decide what the difference is between elegant influencing, recommendation, and selling.
- Authority, belief, and confidence are important (thought too much might make you seem arrogant).
- Understand the power of questions to build bridges.
- Solve problems and get people to where they want to be.
- Avoid jargon, or be prepared to accept they haven't got a clue what you are talking about.
- Learn to love objections, which may not be so; they are often just a search for more information.
- Objections are questions in disguise; they lead to evaluation.
- If you hear, 'That's expensive,' maybe they don't see the value in your proposition.
- When was the last time you phoned clients to thank them?
- Who is better placed to influence people, you or them?
- Read this sentence: 'Don't think of a blue Elephant.' (If you did think of a blue elephant, you have just learned the power of words: we have difficulty processing negatives.)

The Next Steps to Future-Proofing Your Optical Business

Dig deep into your client database.

The answers to most of your problems, and the source of most of your new opportunities, lie here.

Test frequently.

Whatever communication strategies you choose, test them on a small sample and monitor the results. And keep doing it! The most common mistake is having the same recall letter. If you are happy with a 58–68 per cent response rate to a recall letter and a 65 per cent test-dispensing ratio, great. But if you can improve, this you'll have more people buying, and you will have to do less selling!

Assume the sale.

We are wary of assuming anything, but as a mindset, it's important. The people who visit you have forsaken all others, walked past a myriad of doors, chosen not to Internet shop, and have probably had difficulty in parking, so they are prepared to buy from you. If they walk away knowing more than when they arrived, having bought something and learned something, then you've succeeded.

You are good.

You can exceed your clients' expectations, and you can guarantee it.

Smile and be enthusiastic.

Is there anything more contagious? Yes, there is: the lack of either. Here's a thought: How would you treat the very first person who walked through your door on day one of your new business? Here's another thought: How would you treat the very last person you saw, if you knew he was to be the last? Would you thank him?

Certainty and enthusiasm are things people warmly respond to, and if done empathetically, they work well. Faking sincerity is good if you can do it successfully, but most people will see it for what it is.

The Power of Influencing

Influence is about understanding how people react, not manipulating them. People have filters, and when they hear an idea, they will probably react differently. They will almost certainly think differently. Understand this, and you are halfway there. Some people will be big-picture thinkers, and some people will be detail orientated. You cannot speak to them in the same way, but you do have to get them to buy from you. There is no right or wrong approach, only what works.

THE NEXT STEPS TO BUILDING A BETTER OPTICAL BUSINESS

If you want to succeed as an individual or a business, you must develop at least seven talents. You must be able to persuade other people to:

- Do as you want, either face-to-face or in a group.
- Get your boss to believe in you and do what you want.
- Get your colleagues to believe in you and do what you want.
- Get groups of people (large and small) to believe in you and do what you want.
- Get prospective clients to believe in you and buy what you recommend.
- Be inspired by you and follow you.

But above all, you must believe in yourself!

Why Being a Great Optometrist or Dispensing Optician May Not Be Enough

There is a selfish truth about word of mouth (or why referrals don't happen). If referrals really were the panacea most seem to think they are, privately owned businesses would still have the lion's share of the market. They don't, despite having the larger number of doors. So how do we explain the reality?

We have all recommended something at some time to someone, but do we do it every time? Not as much as we like to believe. Whether or not we liked it isn't what motivates us to take the risky step of referring something or someone. Instead, the questions that need to be answered are:

- Do I want to be responsible if my friend has a bad experience?
- Will I get credit if it works, and blame if it doesn't?
- Does sending more business in this direction help me, or does it ultimately make my optician busier or overwhelmed? Or will it encourage them to raise their prices?
- Will my optician be upset with me if the person I recommend acts unpleasantly?
- How will that make me look?
- Is my idea of a great experience different from yours?
- Are my needs simple? Are yours complicated, or do we have a different budget?

- Does it look like I'm getting some sort of backhander or special treatment in exchange? And if so, is that a good thing?

Being really good is merely the first step. In order to earn a referral, you need to make it safe, fun, and worthwhile. You prefer referrals from clients, not from customers.

The Next Steps to Building a Better Optical Business

- Put a formal referral strategy in place, but don't ignore all the other strategies for finding new clients.
- Consider offering some kind of promotional incentive, with real value.
- Give your business card with your direct line number and say, 'Ask your friend to call me.' (Be brave).
- Develop a formal farewell script that can be delivered by any member of staff. (What exactly do you want clients to remember about their visits?)
- Look at your window display. If you think it's difficult, be thankful you are not a pharmacist.
- Don't think your words have any weight? Used carefully, they can move people and change behaviour.

Are You Working in the Business or on the Business?

To discover if we mean you, answer this question. If you took a month off work (unplanned), what would happen to your business?

If your response to the first question is, 'What do you mean?' or, 'It won't function properly,' it means you are working in the business. If you have to take that unplanned month off, and the business gets along just fine without you, then you've been working on the business. You may be the one thing that is stopping your business from reaching its full potential. Scary thought, eh? The situation is not that unusual, because the universities taught you that if you do this, you get that. You are taught to work in the business. You must start to build an optical business that can sack you, or at the very least you can choose the people you want to see.

It might seem impossible to get off the treadmill of routine, the cycle of test, dispense, and recall. But get off it you must, if you are to work on the business and have it work for you, rather than have you work for it. If you think it's difficult to do, it will be, and you won't do it. Try this: Book an appointment with yourself every Friday afternoon from 3–5 p.m. There, it's now in the diary, and your business (happiness) is dictated by the diary and whether or not it's full. Remember Pavlov's dog? You can train yourself. Learning and discovery can be fun. Did you ever go exploring as a child? When did you lose your sense of adventure? Treat yourselves to two hours of fun and stimulation at the end of the week.

If you had an employee who was frustrating your business at every turn, what would you do?

The Next Steps to Building a Better Optical Business

- Adopt, create, borrow, or copy a consistent communication strategy.
- Use your website to attract new clients, educate them, and get them to make appointments.
- Try new ideas. If you aim to try one new idea every two months, you have just developed your first business development plan.
- Don't be afraid of failure. If you were afraid of falling as a child, you'd never have learned to walk.
- Version one is better than version none.
- Remember, we live in a service economy.

Mindset versus State of Mind

What is the difference that makes the difference? Mindset is about striving to become a better influencer, a better communicator. It's about making the complex seem simple, and it will be characterized by the absence of jargon. Learning how to deal with stress and having a positive mental attitude are important – but they may not be enough. How do you think about time? We all have the same amount (if we're lucky). Understanding how people behave is important to mindset. The myth of the work-life balance as the ultimate goal must be dealt with. What's right for you is right. The work-life balance will change, and as likely as not, it will act as a vehicle for change. How you let your past experiences affect your future performance is important.

For the vast majority of people, you are an expert in the unknown (beyond testing eyes and selling specs). So here's a question for you: What business are you really in? Most people do not have an ocular pathology, and neither are they particularly worried about what their eyesight will be like when they reach eighty. Would it surprise you to learn that your business is not about frames and lenses (unless you are happy in the commodity, price sensitive market)? It is more about the result, and it is this that will get you out of commodity pricing so that you will attract the people who pay what you are actually worth.

Here are some questions that will unveil your mindset. What lifestyle do you want to have? What is the biggest challenge you face now? What is worrying you now? If you could wave a magic wand, what would you wish for? Have you ever asked a client, 'What do you want from me?' (That is very different from the excellent question, 'What brings you here today?'). What do you feel vulnerable about? How do you listen to your clients?

Most businesses are stuck (to some degree), or they will be stuck at some point after the initial growth spurt. We are not concerning ourselves with a rapid period of growth due to a new contract, or a new employer or housing estate under development. Growth hides a multitude of sins. We are concerned with what lies beneath. Are you prepared to adopt multiple strategies (rather than sequential ones), and to 'fail fast'? Assume that although your challenge appears to be one thing, accept it might be another thing. There is an alternative story to be told – yours.

A distressed business needs a fast route to profit and then to adopt a mid- to long-term, sustainable growth plan. A very different strategy is required for a fundamentally sound but badly run business, but both will need to be clear about mindset. There are plenty of experts out there telling you that this thing or that thing is what you need to do, and guess what? They have something to sell you. My aim is to tell you about all the things and let you decide. But first things first: get the mindset right and believe. (By the way, you will never know enough.)

You will hear a lot spoken about differentiation or niches, and these are great – but if no one wants what you've got, you don't have a business.

If mindset sounds a bit American and too much like a self-improvement course, think of it in a different way. Imagine a destination, or what you want your business to be like. Never lose sight of that image. Mindset is effectively a road map, a satellite navigation system, a route to get there. There are unlikely to be any ah-ha moments along the way, but there will be way-markers: you will be signing up one more client a week than you lose, your average dispensing value will be increasing by 5–10 per cent, your average test-dispense ratio will be climb steadily by a few percentage points each year, your cost of acquiring a new client will be known, the lifetime value of your client will become the focus of your business, and more clients will make an appointment after receiving the first recall letter.

The Next Steps to Building a Better Optical Business

- Talk is cheap. It's execution that will set you apart.
- Launch fast, fail fast, iterate faster.
- Numbers rule.
- Build a business with a killer culture, not a culture that kills.
- Pick your battles.
- Today's success can breed tomorrow's failure, if success makes you complacent.
- Failure renews your humility, sharpens your objectivity, and makes you more resilient.
- Let 'I will' or 'I must' become your mantra, not 'I'll try'.
- Deal with your fear of failure.
- Say what you think if it serves your purpose.
- Do not take it personally.

Finding the Perfect Client

Imagine your perfect clients; close your eyes and visualise them. They want your products and services – and more important, they value them. They can afford to invest at the level you need to support your business and lifestyle. They understand and appreciate the value you offer, and they tell their friends and families. They are demanding, but they are a pleasure to work with. They listen and understand your suggestions and the reasoning behind your recommendation. They may fit a certain demographic, or they may not.

So, how do you find them, and how do they find you? Is it you they are interested in, or is it what you can do for them? Who decides what they will read next about their eye care? How many times will you have to tell your story before they finally hear it? It's estimated they need to hear what you have to say three to five times before they listen, let alone believe it. If statistics are to be believed, your clients are more likely to survive a plane crash than believe an ad on its first viewing.

If you can visualise your ideal client, then do everything in your power to make it happen. The following suggestions are in no particular order and are far from comprehensive: advertising (online or offline), social media, adopting a formal referral strategy, staff training, putting your prices up, sacking certain customers, choosing different supply partners, renegotiating existing trading terms, exploring a two-tier eye test and examination structure, test a price increase for your sight test fee. Visit the ONS (http://www.ons.gov.uk), a free resource that will tell you more about your town and city than all the accountants, software salespeople, search engines, reps, naysayers, doom mongers, and other experts ever could. If you knew the average wage in the town, how would your prices compare? Are they too high or too low?

Consumers are now more confident, and the old rules are changing. The good news is that it's estimated that 83 per cent of the people you see who have their eye examinations with you will buy their eyewear from you. This is thirty years after they were given the opportunity to choose to take their prescription and buy somewhere else. Here's another thought: with an average of 9,900 people per practice, the UK and Ireland are better placed than most of their European counterparts.

OPTIMISM

For a scientific explanation of optimism, you need you read Tali Sharats's fascinating book, *The Optimism Bias*. Optimism is a mindset, which is very different from your state of mind.

The contention is that optimism is actually hardwired into us. Generally we expect things to turn out for the better, and that optimism inspires and protects us. Optimism requires imaginative or positive thinking and leads to problem solving and discovery. Awareness rarely shatters the illusion. When you know things, you can insulate yourself from the pitfalls, the traps, and the elementary errors. The message is to find out what you don't know and then master it.

Lots of decisions are difficult, but contrast that with having them made for you. Choosing your own outcome often makes us happier. Optimism is also the nearest we can come to time travel. 'Where do you want to be in five years' time?' is a question beloved by limited-thinking interviewers the world over, but when you are building a better optical business, it's a worthwhile thought. The truth is you may not get there by the original path; it may take longer, or you may luck into it sooner. Regardless, the journey of a thousand miles begins with the first step.

OPTIMISATION

Look critically at everything you do, and ask yourself one question: Can it be done better? So, where do you begin? Remember that version one is better than version none, and that having a great theory, vision, or plan is worthless if you don't take action. Before you spend one penny on marketing activities, shop refits, supplier reviews, or other things, do this exercise. It is simple, and it's the most cost effective action you can take. It makes you think and gets you out of the routine mindset. Another way to look at optimization is as a pay raise for you (and your family, and the people who make the magic happen). How often would you choose to give yourself a pay raise?

Optimisation is a continuous process, it becomes part of your killer culture, and it must be hardwired into the DNA of your business. If price sensitivity is where you want to be, fine. But you should really raise your prices regularly over time. Why wait for an annual review?

Something Is Broken. We know It's Broken. Here Are Five Possible Responses

- We can fix it right away and learn from it.
- We fixed it, we don't worry, but we learned nothing – and it will break again. 'I'm just doing my job.'
- We say it's not broken; it is, but we're not willing to admit it.
- We don't know it's broken.
- We may or may not know it's broken, but mostly we don't care enough to try to fix it.

With Whom Are You Competing, and How Are You Competing?

It's easy to understand what you're competing for: sales. But why should people choose you in this post-consumer consumerist society? If you're competing on price, you'll spend most of your time learning about the price of everything and the value of nothing. If you're competing for attention, you'll spend most of your time online, advertising, or developing social media.

Are you competing on trust and keeping the promises that make you trustworthy – and much more important make you be perceived as trustworthy? Competing on qualifications is pointless, because they expect you to be experts. Telling them you are an expert often leads to 'So what?' You invest time getting more CET points, which are professionally fulfilling and a legal requirement. But if you're competing on brands, beware the difference between people who are brand aware and those who are brand driven (and may not be worried about last-season, Internet pricing or performance).

If you're competing by doing faster and cheaper, do it very well, because someone will do it faster and cheaper. If you're competing on innovation, you may be (too far) ahead of the crowd. If you're competing on being independent, be absolutely clear on what that means for your clients, and do everything you can to make it important, relevant, and meaningful.

In any competitive market, be prepared to invest your heart and soul, and focus on the thing you compete on. Choose something you can live with and a practice that allows you to thrive. It's never easy.

ACKNOWLEDGEMENTS

Lots of people were involved in this, most of them unknowingly, so here's a chance to put the record straight. I have had the honour of meeting and in many cases working with some of them. For others, I've met them along the way, or I read or listened to them. To the many people whose company I have enjoyed and who don't appear here: thank you. They are here in no particular order, without their qualifications for the sake of space and brevity.

Frank Norville, John Street, Malcolm Polley, John Conway, Peter Wiles, Mac Mckenna, Simon Johnson, Sheila Walker, Phil Richardson, Kay Jordan, Paul Walden, Paul Hadwin, Robin Hughes, Kelvin Wakefield, Elaine Grisdale, Debbie Gigg, Sue Rose, Sir Anthony Garrett, Michael J. Potter, Alicia Thompson, Paula Stevens, Abi Grute, Mark Nevin, Nick Rumney, Francesca Marchetti, Peter Black, Phil Mullins, David Canton, Tom Goldie, Andy Phillips, Dennis, Dean and Wayne Curcher, Mike Hargreaves, Andy Sanders, Andy Hepworth, Martyn Sales. Nick Atkins, David Goad, Graham Hutchison, Matt Dorling, Isabelle Dekker, David Rips, Igor Loshak, John McCarthy, David Ambler, Ahmad Barzak, Nancy Yamasaki, J. M. Laird, Jantiporl 'Sid' Sidhu, Lino Barbieri, Angelika Fallgren, Jan Krcmar, Alexandra Mullerova, Zuzana Bartonikova, Anita Komarkova Paul Bertolin, Daniel Crespo, Santiago Soler, Javiler Trujillo, Jose-Miguel Cleva, Jose Alonso, Dr Gareth Jones, Alexander Wray Dabell, Trevor Deaves, Mike Chauhan, Simon Aldridge, 'Rico', David Protherough, Adrian Turton, Gareth Warren, Mr Terrington, Simon O' Dwyer Russell, Jodie Cook, Frank Goode, Norman Lovatt, Frances Duncan, Peter Zieman, Mark Robertson, Mike Stewart, Nigel Castle, Scott Pearson, John Taylor, Ray Crofton, Jonathon Bench, Jonathon Winchester. Geoffrey James. Jeff Haden, Frances Duncan, Harry Lumley, Lee Child, Seth Godin, Chris Cardell (and assorted acolytes), Callan Rush, Bernadette Doyle, Tom Searcy, Neil Peart, Ayn

Rand, Thomas Hobbes, John Locke, Nicolai Machiavelli, and Kong Fuzi. I also thank every privately owned lab owner in the UK.

Illustrations are copyright Arnika Müll, ww.arnika-muell.com

And last but not least, thanks to my parents, Christine and David; my brother, Peter; and Fiona, Olivia, and Charles.

ABOUT THE AUTHOR

Julian Wiles grew up in Churchdown, which was then a small village situated between Gloucester and Cheltenham in England. Wiles sold eyeglass frames, optical machines, and lenses for the Norville Group before buying a wholesale lens distribution business with a partner. In 2009, Performance Lenses Ltd. was born. Wiles was also elected vice chair and subsequently chair of the Lens Focus Group.

Printed in the United States
By Bookmasters